THE

BRIDGE

OF

FAITH:

ACCESS TO

THE KINGDOM OF GOD

THE

BRIDGE

OF

FAITH:

ACCESS TO
THE KINGDOM OF GOD

Robert J. Turley

WINEPRESS WP PUBLISHING

Unless otherwise noted all scriptures are taken from the King James Version of the Bible.

Verses marked NASB are taken from the New American Standard Bible, © 1960, 1962, 1963, 1968, 1971, 1972, 1973, 1975, 1977 by The Lockman Foundation. Used by permission.

Verses marked RSV are taken from the Revised Standard Version of the Bible, copyright © 1946, 1952, 1971 by the Division of Christian Education of the National Council of the Churches of Christ in the U.S.A. Used by permission.

Verses marked NRSV are taken from the New Revised Standard Version Bible, copyright © 1989 by the Division of Christian Education of the National Council of the Churches of Christ in the U.S.A. Used by permission. All rights reserved.

Verses marked NAB are taken from The New American Bible, copyright © 1970 by the Confraternity of Christian Doctrine, Washington DC. Used by permission. All rights reserved.

ISBN 1-57921-305-7
Library of Congress Catalog Card Number: 00-102774

To the Spirit of Truth

Who inspired the Scriptures, and

Who even now illuminates their pages

For those who prayerfully seek

His help in reading them.

ACKNOWLEDGMENTS

The longer I live, the more I realize how much I owe to others. This part of his book gives the author the opportunity to tell the world of his gratitude.

I grew up at the tail end of what Tom Brokaw calls "The Greatest Generation." It was in small-town Kentucky during the Great Depression and World War II. I must have been unaware of meanness, because I look back on happy memories about good people.

My father never realized his fondest dreams, perhaps because he died too young. My mother and both widowed grandmothers worked and "kept house"; but that did not keep them from seeing that my siblings, my cousins, and I grew up knowing how to behave, how to respect those in authority, and how to earn what we wanted from life. One of my aunts encouraged my love for books, and the other fed and housed me when I started to university. Both of my uncles were wounded in World War II, one with the Marine Corps in the South Pacific and the other with Patton in Europe. They were heroes.

My family were not the only adults who encouraged and influenced me. My schoolteachers included "Miss Alice" Turner, who taught English and led me to appreciate poetry like "Thanatopsis," the last stanza of which I can still recite from memory. Reverend Olus Hamilton baptized me when I was about 12 or 13 years old. "Miss Anise" Hunt was my Sunday School teacher. She taught me to believe the Bible. My high school principal and debate coach was Professor Kenneth Harding, who taught me to look at both sides of an issue and to think on my feet. William Clay was a lawyer in town. He judged one of my debates and encouraged me to become a lawyer. Lieutenant John Kessler was the Executive Officer of my V-12 Unit who turned down my request for sea duty and made me stay in school. The lawyer for whom I clerked while in law school was kind enough to make me his partner when I graduated. Tom Mooney and I then practiced together until his death. Judge Marsh Porter and Judge Warren Jones gave me opportunities to be of service at the international level of Shriners Hospitals for Children, and Randy Thomas promoted my first election to the Board of Trustees. One of my best friends for many years was Reverend Bob W. Brown. He taught me the importance of people, and the influence we can be on the world.

And these are not all of the wonderfully kind people who helped me through life, but only a representative sample. All those whom I have mentioned have now gone to their reward. I should have paid this tribute to their memory long ago, but better late than never.

I owe so much to so many still living that I cannot name them all. However, with a focus on their help with *The Bridge of Faith*, I would like to acknowledge with gratitude the fact that two ministers of the gospel, Dr. Adron Doran and Dr. Richard Landon, very kindly read the manuscript in draft and offered suggestions which I consider very valuable. My secretary, Pamela Gieringer, did her usual stellar job of holding the whole manuscript together during the many drafts and re-drafts produced by my obsessive compulsiveness. Finally, I am again grateful to my special friend, Susan Graves Tebbs, for her patience and encouragement during the ups and downs of producing *The Bridge of Faith*.

I am forever in debt to these, both living and dead, as well as to many others who have been sources of strength and support for me for many, many years.

—LEXINGTON, KENTUCKY
JUNE 2000

C O N T E N T S

FOREWORD

Those who seem reluctant to answer an invitation to "come to Jesus" may be mistakenly thought to have already made some essential preliminary decisions, when they have not yet done so. The purpose of this book is to examine those essential premises upon which the Christian invitation rests.

No agnostic can feel any need for salvation via a Messiah. "Salvation from what?" he demands. The atheist looks only to himself for his purpose in life, both as an individual and in his relationships with others. So the first task of an evangelist is to guide the unbeliever out of his self-centeredness into recognition of a world where he can acknowledge an intelligent and purposeful Creator.

The harmony of nature and its laws, the magic of the seed, the surges and limits of growth, the marvels discovered by science, and the evident scope of human intelligence all make the most compelling argument for purposeful creation and meaning to life. Reason tells us that all these things we see about us cannot have "just happened"; nor can they have grown from nothingness, of their own volition. So reason leads us to believe that there was a "first source," a creator. We call that creator God.

Multitudes of men must live in limited time and space— with each other. Even the least thoughtful of us can see from his own experience that men are happier when they live with each other in harmony and that their relationships with each other bear heavily on their own peace of mind. He can likewise see that he has the freedom to hate and harm his fellows; and they him. The Creator has given his creature the freedom and dignity to make choices, even choices with harmful consequences to himself and others. In this Eden, God has given human beings freedom of choice—even freedom to mess it up.

We can likewise see that peace and harmony are the result of love and that love requires one to look outside himself to see and serve the needs of others. But egocentricity is the antithesis of love; so those who are self-centered are blind to love.

God saw the selfishness of men; and he knew that to keep the strong from devouring the weak, in the absence of love, there must be law to serve as a substitute for love. Law would not be needed if men's relations with each other were grounded in love. No doubt this is the reason for the two "greatest" Commandments; i.e., that one love God and love one's neighbor.

What Christians call "conviction of sin" is simply a person's realization that he has fallen short of the standards of his Creator, in his own life and in his relationships with other people. He understands that he has consumed his life with self-centeredness, and thereby failed miserably in showing love for God and others. This "conviction" invariably concerns specific wrongs done to others; and, consequently, wrongs before God. It drives the need for confession that he has been captive of his self, chained by his own pride, lust and greed, and thereby restrained from seeing and serving the needs of others. In a word, he comes to realize that his egocentricity itself separates him from God. His self-centeredness is the fertile ground in which sin thrives.

Intuitively, and even if he cannot articulate the reasons for his knowing so, man knows that he deserves punishment for his sins. He surely wants mercy; and he can, no doubt, persuade himself in many ways that he deserves mercy. But, deep in his heart of hearts, he knows that he deserves punishment. Not only so, he feels guilt. He searches for excuses and clings to every one; but he still feels guilt. Shame destroys his peace of mind.

Any human being who has come this far knows his need for forgiveness; but he may not know how to have forgiveness and, with it, peace of mind as well as eternal life.

Over the centuries and throughout the world people have felt the overwhelming need to look outside themselves for purpose, power and peace. Their search has been limited only by their imagination. Some have created idols, their own handmade objects of worship. Others have looked for a revelation of the Creator in creation itself, or in "signs" or in the "magic" of their medicine men.

From the fertile crescent of the Middle East came monotheism, one God known as Yahweh or Jehovah. He was the God of Abraham, Isaac, and Jacob. Through the patriarchs, the Pentateuch, the Psalms and the prophets, this one God revealed himself and claimed allegiance to himself alone. He gave his followers laws by which to live, and Moses clearly told them that the laws were for their own good. But over generations, self-centeredness led them to have greater concern for the letter of the law and its outward manifestations than for its spirit and the attitude of love that underlies its requirements. They first satisfied themselves and then tried to please God with sacrificed animals, rather than through service to each other in his name.

So they disobeyed the God who had created them; and they shunned his way.

We know this because we read it in the Bible. The Bible is history, but not just a history of *what* happened *where* and *when*. The Bible is a history of God's revelation of himself to humankind—a history of *why*. It is about God who is spirit, transcendent, eternal. Not being material and not confined to time and space, God is not subject to comprehension by reason alone. So the Bible can be rightly read and interpreted only with the aid of the Spirit of Truth.[1]

The Christian gospel has it that this same God, out of his everlasting lovingkindness and grace, provided his own Son as the only acceptable sacrifice to take away the sins of all those who would turn away from their sin, ask forgiveness, and follow him. He was Jesus, the Christ, the Messiah of whom the prophets had told. He was an incomparable teacher and the sinless example of God incarnate. Yet few would believe him, and the religious leaders of his people had him crucified. Too many held on to their self-centered ways and turned away from love.

That this Jesus is truly the Son of God, like that God himself is the "First Cause," can be apprehended only by faith. No man can be shown physical evidence which he cannot question. He must believe something he cannot see. Yet there are eyewitnesses who told of having seen Jesus risen from the dead. These eyewitnesses, who had run away in fear before his death, stood boldly before kings and judges after his resurrection, sublimely confident in him as their Savior.

So it is that those who will admit to sin can now find forgiveness, if they will believe and follow Jesus. The way is clear. He said to them all:

> If any man will come after me, let him deny himself, and take up his cross daily, and follow me. For whosoever will save his life shall lose it: but whosoever will lose his life for my sake, the same shall save it.[2]

So in following Jesus, the promise of God becomes the peace of God.[3]

CREATION:
LIFE AND PURPOSE

F rom earliest recorded history, men have asked questions we have come to classify as religious or philosophical. These include: "Who am I? Where do
humans come from? Where are we going? What is the
purpose?"

Philosophers and religionists have proposed many different answers to these questions, depending upon their
assumptions and their methods. Scientists and rationalists
of the "age of enlightenment" in the seventeenth and eigh-
teenth centuries laid the groundwork for Charles Darwin's
theory of evolution, about which he wrote in the nineteenth
century. So arose the dichotomy between those who believe in creation and those who believe in evolution. Even
though some would not draw the line so clearly (and argue
that creation itself was by means of evolution) the ultimate
issue remains: "Was there a Creator?"

"Creationists" today decry the teaching of evolution in
the public schools, as if it were established truth and without a balanced presentation of creation. Their opponents

claim that creation is only myth. Virtually all religion and philosophy may trace its rationale to the original issue: "Was the universe created?"

According to the creationists, God created the material universe out of nothing, and all else follows from that fact. The evolutionists begin with a universe already in existence or a "big boom" and cannot go behind that. Either they can express no first premise or they simply assume the appearance of something out of nothing without a cause. James S. Trefil says:

> How it began, no one is quite sure. The evidence strongly suggests, however, that a tiny fraction of a second after the moment of its creation, our universe consisted of a dense, rapidly expanding collection of matter.[1]

Following that "suggestion," the author speaks of some happenings only split seconds apart and others separated by billions of years, as if he really knew. He passes off science fiction as fact; so more and more people who know no better are led to believe that scientists really know the truth.[2] The word "creation" is not even indexed in his book. Our thesis here is that meaning of life can be sought only in relation to its beginning, which was by creation.

As has been said by one of the Romans in writing to his son: "Before entering into or upon the systematic discussion of any subject, we must first define our terms." When we speak of creation, we use the following definitions:

Creationism: The belief that God created the heavens, the earth, and all living things.

Deism: Belief, based solely on reason, in the existence of God as the creator of the universe who, after setting it in motion, abandoned it, assumed no control over life, exerted no influence on natural phenomena, and gave no supernatural revelation.[3]

Theism: Belief in the existence of a god or gods, especially belief in a personal God as creator and ruler of the world.[4]

Monotheism: The doctrine or belief that there is only one God.[5]

Rationalism: The theory that the exercise of reason, rather than the acceptance of empiricism, authority, or spiritual revelation, provides the only valid basis for action or belief, and that reason is the prime source of knowledge and of spiritual truth.[6]

Supernatural: Attributed to a power that seems to violate or go beyond natural laws; miraculous. Of or pertaining to a deity.[7]

Spiritual: Of, from, or pertaining to God; deific.[8]

Spirit: The vital principle or animating force traditionally believed to be within living beings.. . . The essential nature of a person.[9]

The question, stated as if for high school debating teams, is "RESOLVED: the heavens and the earth, together with the living plants, animals and mankind were and are the result of a creative mind and force called God." One may argue either the affirmative or the negative of that proposition. "Religionists" take the affirmative. "Rationalists" take the negative. I choose the affirmative because I believe it to be truth.

Consideration of abstract ideas appropriately begins with consideration of matters which are known to exist and can be observed or otherwise perceived by the senses.[10] If we are to consider the issue of creation, and all that follows

THE BRIDGE OF FAITH

from an acceptance of creation as truth, we should begin with an inventory of the material things that somehow came into being. If we suggest as a conclusion that the material world was created, we can look to the material world for some evidence to support that conclusion.

First, we know that the material universe is subject to the "laws" of time and space, and to the "laws" of force and motion, and to other "laws of nature." We can observe the evidence of these "laws," and even measure their effect in given circumstances. They affect us in a multitude of ways. While science intensely studies these "laws," it has not yet exhausted its examination. Indeed, there remains great mystery about these matters, and science may never be able to answer all its questions. These "laws" are so complex that only experts have more than a basic knowledge of their effect.

Second, we can observe material "things" which can be counted, weighed, and measured but have no life or energy in themselves. These are materials such as stones, soil, and water. They are useful, of course; but their usefulness is dependent upon their reaction to outside forces such as light, heat, or chemicals. Their usefulness to us is related to the "laws" of nature.

Third, we see living plants that are inanimate or rooted. Through the magic of the seed, coupled with the fertility of nutrients in the soil, plants can reproduce themselves when given the benefit of light, water, and sometimes heat. These various natural forces work together in ways studied by scientists, but still not fully understood by them.

Animals, like plants, are life-infused and reproductive. They are not rooted but mobile, so they can utilize instinct to find food, reproduce themselves, and in turn provide food for others in the "food chain" of nature. Many of them socialize with others of their species. Some of them migrate long distances with changes of the seasons. Some can be domesticated and trained to comply with the wishes of men.

Finally, we have humankind, with physical and chemical characteristics similar to those of plants and animals, but with intellect and the power to reason abstractly. We know of mutations in plants and animals, some of which have been initiated by man. But only mankind has developed from "hunter/gatherer" to farmer to mechanic to professional to philosopher. Only mankind has designed systems of communication, transportation, and commerce. Only mankind has produced legal systems and governments to meet social needs. Only mankind is partially civilized. Only mankind can initiate and foster science, so as to employ the laws of nature and utilize to his own benefit the earth, its plants, and animals. And only mankind can ask the question: "Was the material world and man himself *created*?"

I look at my hand as I write this book, and I see only one complex member of a body with myriad systems for sensation, action, nourishment, healing, cogitation, and reproduction. All of these systems work together; and, while they age and one or more sometimes fails, the design of man's anatomy and physiology is mind-boggling. So, too, are nature's laws. I cannot find it credible that humankind and this intricate material world in which we live are the result of mindless chance, or evolution alone, without any design at the beginning. Such a conclusion is wholly unbelievable; and I firmly reject it. It would require an unsupportable rationale, contrary to much of the evidence, born of theory, surmise and guess.

After beginning his chapter with a quotation from Schopenhauer, viz., "To believe that physical and chemical forces could by themselves bring about an organism is not merely mistaken but, as already remarked, stupid," the eminent scientist, Brian L. Silver, goes on to confess:

I do not know the origin of life. Those of us who hold, like I do, that life emerged spontaneously from inanimate matter are, we must admit, at a distinctly embarrassing disadvantage: we have not yet come up with a convincing mechanism for abiogenesis.[11]

Fair consideration of the evidence we can apprehend by our senses and comprehend by our intellect leads me to believe that the Bible truly states the facts when it says:

In the beginning God created the heaven and the earth . . .[12]

So God created man in his own image, in the image of God created he him; male and female created he them.[13]

It must be clearly understood that the issue here is *whether* God created, not *when* or *how* he did so.

Even the intellectuals who deny a Creator must begin somewhere, and their theories beg the question. As Dr. Silver writes:

Those scientists concerned with the origins of the physical universe begin their investigations just after the Creation, not just before. . . .

When we speak of the Big Bang theory, we are speaking of a family of theories, differing from each other on a variety of issues but all accepting the general picture of an initial cataclysmic creation of "something" about 15 billion years ago, followed by a furious expansion.[14]

One is tempted to argue with scientists upon their own ground; but any such argument is futile because monotheism's God is spiritual, not material. Argument in material terms concerning God, a spirit, is counterproductive and foolish.

It is like two people arguing with each other; one in a foreign language the other neither understands nor accepts as legitimate.

Reason is not enough to grasp spiritual matters, and God is spirit. Only by faith may one apprehend spiritual matters. While the atheist says: "Seeing is believing," the monotheistic Jew, Christian, and Muslim all say, "Believing is seeing." The Bible says:

> God is a spirit; and they that worship Him must worship Him in spirit and in truth.[15]

This is very difficult for the rationalist and the intellectual. For them the pride of intellect gets in the way of faith. But Jesus said that we must "become as little children."[16] If God were grasped only by intellect, most of us could never know him. We are simply not smart enough to comprehend the spirit of God. Yet even a child can *believe*. There is a chasm between pure reason and the spiritual world; and faith is the bridge which leads from reason to the spiritual.

That being the case, we can confidently look to the Bible as a means used by God to reveal the truth of creation through the patriarchs,[17] psalmists,[18] and prophets.[19] Jesus likewise attributed creation to God.[20] There are those who believe that the Genesis account of creation in six days is an ancient myth repeated to generation after generation until finally reduced to writing, and that it was never to be taken literally to mean six twenty-four hour days. Even they insist that to quibble about the "time" it took God to effect the creation—long before there were clocks or calendars—is to miss the point. The point is that God created everything but himself; and that he did so with a plan and a purpose.

Margaret Nutting Ralph teaches the Bible as literature, approaching it as books by different authors using several different literary forms. She treats the creation story in

Genesis as "myth" after having carefully explained that "myth is not a synonym for fiction."[21] She defines myth as "an imaginative story which uses symbols to speak about reality, but a reality which is beyond a person's comprehension," and explains that "societies compose myths to orient themselves in a moral and spiritual world."[22]

Stanley Grenz tells us that the Bible is the work of the Holy Spirit using human hands; and that, as the Spirit was in the writing by "inspiration," so the Spirit can be in the reading by "illumination."[23] The Bible can be properly interpreted only with the aid of the Spirit of Truth, not by historians such as John Dominic Crossan who begin with a firmly held pre-judgment that there is no such thing as a miracle,[24] and who confine their consideration to what they can "prove" by speculation, guess, and supposition. To read the Bible without the aid of the Spirit is like trying to win the Indy 500 in a car with the brakes locked, or the Kentucky Derby with a 500-pound jockey.

Could Holy Scripture contain myth? Could the written Word of God include "symbols to speak about reality"? For answer, turn to the Bible itself; and, specifically, to the words of Jesus. Again and again he taught in parables, allegory, and metaphor. He told his disciples that he taught in parables because he could use the stories to illustrate spiritual truth for them.[25]

So whether the Genesis creation story is a myth handed down from generation to generation and ultimately written is really beside the point. The point is: Can we believe that God created the heavens and the earth? Except for insatiably curious cosmologists or some demented person who wants to replicate creation, details such as time and mode are of little interest. The lesson we should draw from Genesis is that man and his environment are the product of a purposeful design and production, hence by God.

Believing that God created us, intuitively we know that he had a purpose for creation. As his creatures, we must look to our Creator for the purpose of our own lives, all in the context that our lives—in terms of our time, talents and resources—are his products. This is to say that God gives breath to our newly born bodies and then says: "Here's your toolbox. Build a life. Use my plan and build on a solid foundation." The Bible confirms our intuitive belief that God has a purpose for each life. It says through the Apostle Paul:

> . . . let each of you lead the life that the Lord has assigned, to which God called you.[26]

We also read of God's purpose for Jacob,[27] for Pharaoh,[28] for Nebuchadnezzar,[29] for Jesus,[30] for Paul[31] and for the saints at Ephesus.[32]

As for God's overall purpose and its execution, Paul writes to the Ephesians that:

> Blessed be the God and Father of our Lord Jesus Christ, who has blessed us in Christ with every spiritual blessing in the heavenly places, just as he chose us in Christ before the foundation of the world to be holy and blameless before him in love. He destined us for adoption as his children through Jesus Christ, according to the good pleasure of his will, to the praise of his glorious grace that he freely bestowed on us in the Beloved. In him we have redemption through his blood, the forgiveness of our trespasses, according to the riches of his grace that he lavished on us.
>
> With all wisdom and insight he has made known to us the mystery of his will, according to his good pleasure that he set forth in Christ, as a plan for the fullness of time, to gather up all things in him, things in heaven and things on earth. In Christ we have also obtained an inheritance, having been destined accord-

ing to the purpose of him who accomplishes all things according to his counsel and will . . .[33]

Paul also wrote to Timothy about God's purpose and grace, saying:

> Do not be ashamed, then, of the testimony about our Lord or of me his prisoner, but join with me in suffering for the gospel, relying on the power of God, who saved us and called us with a holy calling, not according to our works but according to his own purpose and grace.[34]

And, finally, in writing to the Romans he said:

> We know that all things work together for good for those who love God, who are the called according to his purpose.[35]

So it was with Joseph, after his brothers had sold him as a slave to the Egyptians and years later found him as governor, in charge of the food they had come from Canaan to buy. He later said to his brothers:

> But as for you, ye thought evil against me: but God meant it unto good, to bring to pass, as it is this day, to save much people alive.[36]

We sometimes see part of God's plan in hindsight; but, even then, we can never see the whole. Perhaps his plan for mankind is like the picture on a jigsaw puzzle box, not furnished to us now. We have the pieces of the puzzle—all different shapes and colors—but no picture on top of the box. However, the directions are clear: find a way to fit the pieces together using shapes and colors of truth and love and service. Then someday we will see that these different shapes and colors will fit together into a beautiful awe-inspiring whole. To avoid frustration now, we need faith and patience.

So we are not deists, but theists and, more specifically, monotheists who believe in a designed and perfectly executed creation by a loving God who had (and has) a plan for mankind, which someday shall be revealed in all its glory. This earth is neither heaven nor hell, nor was it meant to be solely suffering or solely bliss. It is the learning place, the preparation place, the place for choices, freely made, which will determine the ultimate and eternal destiny of each of us. Here each human being is free to choose whether or not he will serve God's purpose or his own.

As evidence of his purpose for each of us, God has given us talents related to a specific "calling" or purpose. Paul deals with this in his first letter to the Corinthians when he writes about their spiritual gifts. He writes, metaphorically, of how they differ as the members of a body differ, each to serve its own purpose so that the body can perform its different functions. Then he relates all to God's purpose:

> But as it is, God arranged the members in the body, each one of them, as he chose.[37]

Paul's point is that each person should serve God's purpose for his life with the talents he has been given, which differ from those given to other people.

Oswald Chambers said it in this way:

> There is only one relationship that matters, and that is your personal relationship to a personal Redeemer and Lord. Let everything else go, but maintain that at all costs, and God will fulfil His purpose through your life. One individual life may be of priceless value to God's purposes, and yours may be that life.[38]

Indeed, we are stewards of all our resources: our time, talent, and means. These resources are to be used in service, which is God's overall purpose for each and all of us.

Your place and method of service may be identified by your opportunities. Those are the doors that open to you. Others in like manner identify their own callings.

> Whether numbered with peasants or counted
> with kings,
>
> Your life has a purpose in God's system
> of things.
>
> Appraise your abilities, and there find a
> clue
>
> To the purpose for which God created you.
>
> What course has he charted for your life
> to take?
>
> What door does he open? What circum-
> stance make?
>
> Your life is a mission for you to
> fulfill,
>
> Using all your ability, talent and skill.

This being the case, we are to give up control of ourselves and our resources to God's purpose for our lives as opportunities present themselves. The alternative is self-centeredness, which looks attractive but doesn't truly satisfy. Instead, self-centeredness produces slavery to sin, frustration, futility, and wasted lives.

If we freely enlist our lives and resources to God's service, without being "drafted" or serving in a rebellious attitude, we shall have the peace that "passeth understanding." Then every life will have a steeple reaching to God, with a cross on top to show its ownership in him.

CHAPTER TWO

FREEDOM OF WILL
AND CHOICE

K arl Barth makes the case concerning the freedom
of God, and the freedom of man.[1] With but short
concentrated thought, we can conclude that God
is free—free to determine his own nature and character—
unconstrained by any other spirit or power—completely
free.

In that freedom, God chose to be truth, without any
falsehood or error about himself. In that freedom, God chose
for himself those attributes by which we identify him: justice, grace, light, mercy and love—for examples. And by
those choices he denied to his nature and character the
contrary, such as: tyranny, meanness, and evil of whatever
kind. God chose to be love, and there can be no relationship with God apart from love.

No doubt God could have chosen to make each one of
us a robot or puppet. In such case, we would have no wills
of our own. We would be as submissive as well-tamed and
domesticated animals. But he chose another course. At his

instance, each of us has a place and a purpose in God's overall plan.

The scriptures tell us that God made man in his own image.[2] That being so, he endowed man with freedom. God gave man free will, freedom of choice, freedom to make his own decisions. Even after Israel was given the Law through Moses, and God commanded obedience as a condition to his covenant with them, God recognized their free will, saying through Moses:

> I call heaven and earth to witness against you today, that I have set before you life and death, the blessing and the curse. So choose life in order that you may live, you and your descendants, . . . [3]

In the Wisdom of Sirach, it is said:

> When God, in the beginning, created man, he made him subject to his own free choice.
> If you choose you can keep the commandments; it is loyalty to do his will.
> There are set before you fire and water; to whichever you choose, stretch forth your hand.
> Before man are life and death, whichever he chooses shall be given him.[4]

A present-day student of Augustine tells us that "Augustine's universe operates exclusively by the will of God, and his focus is on developing a conception of free will that is consistent with total dependence of human beings on God and yet that preserves the goodness and justice of God in punishing sinners." He goes on to quote from Augustine himself as follows:

. . . What was not done by will would be neither evildoing nor right action. Both punishment and reward would be unjust if man did not have free will. Moreover, there must needs be justice both in punishment and in reward, since justice is one of the goods that are from God. Therefore, God must needs have given free will to man. (*Free Choice*. II. 1.5–7)[5]

Barth puts it this way in his essay on "The Gift of Freedom":

Human freedom is the *gift* of God in the free outpouring of his grace. To call a man free is to recognize that God has *given* him freedom.[6]

But he goes on to say:

. . . The source of man's freedom is also its yardstick. . . . Sin as an alternative is not anticipated or included in the freedom given to man by God. . . . Sinful man is not free, he is a captive, a slave.[7]

Next question: What do we humans do with this gift of freedom? The universal answer is that we start out life completely self-centered. Regrettably, some are never otherwise. Most proceed from focus on self to some focus on extensions of self—our kin and our things. We call this love; but it is only possessive.

As some people grow up, they begin to mature and to look outside themselves. Their maturity can lead to recognition of the spiritual element of life. The next step is to realize that there is a Creator whom we call God. From that point on, the issue is one of choice between selfish and material interests on the one hand and spiritual values and principles on the other.

God is good. He is righteous. So even though man is given free will, the God of righteousness cannot condone unrighteousness. Before Moses was given the Law, men made in the image of God—through reason and even intuitively—knew there was a difference between good and evil. Paul explained that to the Romans, saying:

> For since the creation of the world His invisible attributes, His eternal power and divine nature, have been clearly seen, being understood through what has been made, so that they (that is, men) are without excuse. For even though they knew God, they did not honor Him as God, or give thanks; but they became futile in their speculations, and their foolish heart was darkened. Professing to be wise, they became fools, and exchanged the glory of the incorruptible God for an image in the form of corruptible man and of birds and four-footed animals and crawling creatures.[8]

Man can freely choose to imitate the character of God or to shun it.

> One of the most desperate quests of our time is for personal identity.[9]

We look in all the wrong places: money, power, position, popularity, recognition, i.e., to be "somebody." The basic premise of life—from which all choices and decisions should be made—is this: God created each of us with a purpose of his own. Everything flows from that fact; and use of a life for other than God's purpose is consistent with free will but inconsistent with a true and fruitful "personal identity."

A reasonably thoughtful person sooner or later faces the question: "Who am I?" His answer must be related to his resources, the least of which include time, talents, and intellect. After an inventory of his resources, he may then choose to waste them, to misuse them, or to use them in an appropriate and effective way. That brings him to his next question, which is, "What is the right and proper way?" This question may also be put as, "What is the purpose of my life?" Each of us must answer that question for himself, of course; but upon the answer will depend the course of his life and his destiny in the hereafter.

One of the world's great lay Christian apologists, G. K. Chesterton, provided an example we can easily understand. Here is his "theorem":

> . . . According to most philosophers, God in making the world enslaved it. According to Christianity, in making it, he set it free. God had written, not so much a poem, but rather a play; a play he had planned as perfect, but which had necessarily been left to human actors and stage managers, who had since made a great mess of it.[10]

Later Chesterton writes:

> All Christianity concentrates on the man at the cross-roads.

• • •

> But the point is that a story is exciting because it has in it so strong an element of will, of what theology calls free will. You cannot finish a sum how you like. But you can finish a story how you like. . . . And Christendom has excelled in the narrative romance exactly because it has insisted on the theological free will. . . . [11]

Freedom of choice implies alternatives from which the choices will be made. One must recognize that choices have consequences; and standards or values must be taken into account. Even if one's choice is between two alternatives, both of which are advantageous to himself, he must weigh the consequences of each alternative in order to determine which he believes to be the better. Quite obviously, there may be more than two alternatives. One or more may require self-discipline or self-sacrifice, and the consequences of each may be difficult to predict. Commercial decisions are often based on what is called a "risk benefit analysis." Here, however, we are considering freedom of choice that has ethical and moral implications, rather than simply commercial ends.

There are many who would say that this present is a wicked and perverse generation which worships gods of its own making and which turns values upside down. In the name of "freedom" or "rights", it re-defines standards of morality. Every bodily temptation—whether sex, money, ego, or creature comfort—is treated as acceptable and used as a premise by advertisers to sell more and more "consumer goods." The Ten Commandments are banned from schools and public places in the name of "diversity," and "separation of church and state." Abortion is promoted as "the woman's right to choose." A Bible-carrying President seduces or is seduced by a young intern, and then sticks his finger in the face of the people to lie to them about it. Even after he is proven to have lied under oath, great numbers of people support him nonetheless because they consider his adultery to be a "private matter"—and "the economy is good."[12]

Those who do or defend evil tend to call it by another name; to use distortion, deception, or half-truth. Sometimes

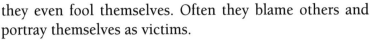

they even fool themselves. Often they blame others and portray themselves as victims.

Those who name evil by its true name are called "self-righteous" and told they dare not "cast the first stone." Must the innocent look away to not "judge" the liar and cheat? Does freedom of choice justify wrong? May the community not protect itself from thieves and killers? Has it no recourse against one who bears false witness? Or may one under oath choose the subjects as to which he will tell "the truth, the whole truth, and nothing but the truth," and lie about other subjects?

If we are to recognize good, we must necessarily recognize evil.

Even Peter observed that Paul's letters were sometimes hard to understand,[13] but Paul certainly wrote with clarity and specificity to the Romans, when he wrote:

> For the wrath of God is revealed from heaven against all ungodliness and wickedness of men who by their wickedness suppress the truth. For what can be known about God is plain to them, because God has shown it to them. . . . Therefore God gave them up in the lusts of their hearts to impurity, to the dishonoring of their bodies among themselves, because they exchanged the truth about God for a lie and worshiped and served the creature rather than the Creator, who is blessed for ever! Amen. For this reason God gave them up to dishonorable passions. . . . [14]

We believe that God communicates with us. Maybe not in the way he spoke to Moses from a bush that burned but was not consumed; maybe not from a blinding light like he spoke to Saul on the road to Damascus, nor even in a still small voice, as to Elijah. But we believe he speaks to us, and often very clearly. He speaks to us through the Bible, through circumstances, through the testimony and influence of others, through prayer, and through the Holy Spirit. Sometimes he speaks to us through suffering—ours or that of somebody else. But one must *listen*, and *believe*. Selective hearing is deafness to his word. Distractions, unbelief, "worldliness" or materialism, and self-centeredness are all used by Satan to create "static" and interference with God's message to us. One can see and not comprehend, hear and not understand— all for the lack of attention and thoughtful reflection.

As a part of his communication with his creatures, God defined the principles by which men can live with each other in harmony.

The same God who gave mankind freedom of choice also gave us standards and values, some of which we know as the Ten Commandments or the Law. Law is the cement by which a community can be bound together; and, at the same time, it is the lubricant by which people with differing interests can live together with the least amount of friction. So God gave Israel the law for its own good and benefit. And, through Moses, God told them that he expected them to obey the law, which was a condition to the covenant by which he promised them the "land of milk and honey".

It is one thing to obey the letter of the law with no motivation other than fear of punishment. It is quite another thing to obey the spirit of the law out of a sense of respect and love for the Lawgiver. Through Jeremiah, God promised a new covenant by which he would write the law in the hearts of his people.[15] Speaking through Ezekiel, the Lord said:

> A new heart also will I give you, and a new spirit will I put within you; and I will take away the stony heart out of your flesh, and I will give you a heart of flesh. And I will put my spirit within you, and cause you to

walk in my statutes, and ye shall keep my judgments, and do them.[16]

So it was that Paul could write to the Corinthians concerning his ministry to them, saying:

> . . . our sufficiency is of God; who also hath made us able ministers of the new testament; not of the letter, but of the spirit: for the letter killeth, but the spirit giveth life.[17]

The explanation Paul gave to the Corinthians was not unlike that which he wrote to the Romans. He reminded the Romans that their justification before God was by faith through God's grace; not by their living within the letter of the law. He told them: "being justified by faith, we have peace with God through our Lord Jesus Christ".[18] To the Corinthians he had written:

> All things are lawful unto me, but all things are not expedient; all things are lawful for me, but I will not be brought under the power of any.[19]

> All things are lawful for me, but all things are not expedient; all things are lawful for me, but all things edify not.[20]

This is to say that, under the new covenant, Christians are expected to freely choose to please God. So will their focus be on love of God and love of neighbor, rather than upon the letter of the law. Love is the spirit of the law. To sum it up, the Apostle wrote:

> For, brethren, ye have been called unto liberty; only use not liberty for an occasion to the flesh, but by love serve

one another. For all the law is fulfilled in one word, even in this; thou shalt love thy neighbor as thyself.[21]

And elsewhere:

Owe no man any thing, but to love one another: for he that loveth another hath fulfilled the law.[22]

Choices proceed from one's motivation, and motivation can be driven by body, mind or spirit. The body has needs and appetites, any of which can be satisfied by good or evil. For example, one can eat to live or live to eat. The one is healthy, and the other is gluttony. The mind is the seat of intellect. Through knowledge, memory, and thought, the mind provides the intellectual basis for accommodation to one's environment, for his activity and for relationships to other people. The spirit is the seat of the emotions and the will. Sometimes called "the heart," it is the seat of faith and love. It is that part of the person which motivates him at the deepest level.

As someone has said: life is like a car, it is driven from the inside out. In the absence of some outside force or disease, the spirit and the mind usually work together to make the choices which direct the body's actions. Together the spirit and the mind comprehend wisdom and virtue; and it is they which adopt one's values or standards of behavior. Given a sense of values and standards of behavior, right or wrong can be discerned by either the intellect (through reason) or the spirit (through conscience). But it is the spirit that chooses love as motivation, because the mind alone is self-centered and inward-directed. Hold to the "good-hearted" and beware the intelligent but mean-spirited.

Choices have consequences. Sometimes the consequences are immediate, and sometimes delayed. Often both.

Sometimes the consequences affect only the actor, and sometimes others. Often both. Here, we are concerned with consequences that are both temporal and eternal.

The Psalmist's is the voice of God as to the consequences of disobedience. It is written:

> But My people did not listen to My voice; and Israel did not obey Me. So I gave them over to the stubbornness of their heart, to walk in their own devices. Oh that My people would listen to Me, that Israel would walk in My ways! I would quickly subdue their enemies, and turn My hand against their adversaries. Those who hate the Lord would pretend obedience to Him; and their time of punishment would be forever. But I would feed you with the finest of the wheat; and with honey from the rock I would satisfy you.[23]

It is this freedom of choice, this freedom to disobey, which carries with it responsibility for the consequences of disobedience. That is why nearly 100 years ago Chesterton wrote:

> . . . this is the real objection to that torrent of modern talk about treating crime as a disease, about making a prison merely a hygienic environment like a hospital, of healing sin by slow scientific methods. The fallacy of the whole thing is that evil is a matter of active choice whereas disease is not. [24]

With free will comes the duty to make proper choices. In other words, man *must* choose. He *cannot* serve both God and mammon. This is why Joshua said to the children of Israel, "Choose you this day whom ye will serve, . . . but as for me and my house, we will serve the Lord".[25] It is an awesome responsibility, this freedom of choice—to choose right or to choose wrong—and to be accountable for our choices and their consequences. But make no mistake about it, each of us bears that awesome responsibility for himself.

Barth goes on in his explanation of human freedom to say:

> Human freedom is the God-given freedom to obey. . . . This obedience confirms and evinces the transition from sin to righteousness, from the flesh to the spirit, from the law to the sovereignty of the living God, from death to life in the small and preliminary, yet determined steps of the daily journey.[26]

In his freedom, God could have called off the whole of humanity as being a failure—not his failure, but the failure of free mankind to choose a character compatible with that of God himself. How could God want to spend eternity with any man or woman who rejected him during a lifetime here on earth and freely chose a character and behavior which are the antithesis of the nature and character of God? Yet out of his everlasting lovingkindness and abundant grace, he chose instead to provide a way for man's salvation and to offer it to any man who would repent and believe. So came Jesus. So also after the freedom to sin came the free choice of salvation for those who would admit their guilt, and, in faith, turn back to God.

CHAPTER THREE

EDEN AND THE
ISSUE OF SUFFERING

We who credit God with creation are first-off faced with a question from those who doubt that fact. The question is: "If God created the world, why is there suffering?" To the honest inquirer, any creationist owes an honest reply. Following is mine.

First, I confess that there is no one comprehensive, easy answer. But there are several answers, depending on the specifics of the suffering. Even so, there are cases in which the answer is beyond our knowledge, and this we must admit. The skeptic may demand that he be convinced by complete and unassailable answers, but an honest inquirer can accept answers which are beyond a reasonable doubt.

To try to understand this issue we must first accept some premises from which we may then draw logical conclusions. I suggest the following premises:

- *God created the heavens and the earth.* Without that assumption, to question God is nonsense. One cannot question the actions of a God he believes does not exist. To deny that there was a Creator just because there is suffering is to beg the question. So, at least for the sake of argument, the inquirer must accept that premise.

- *There are some forces of nature.* These, such as "laws of force and motion," have effects related to the earth's rotation and its atmosphere. These and other natural laws are part of the design of our environment, created for man's good and for his use.

- *Man was given intellect and freedom of choice.* He can use his environment for the benefit of himself and others, or to their detriment, depending on his choices.

- *Man's actions have consequences*, for himself and for others, sometimes for good and sometimes for harm. This is true even when his actions are thoughtless or careless, as well as when they are intentional or purposeful.

- *Plants, animals and man grow and then age; and life in this world ends in death.* We can see many reasons why the nature of matter and its decay make death a positive and beneficial end of this earthly existence, and only the foolish would want to live in this world forever. Without death there would not be space or food or opportunity for the newly born. So there is a beneficial natural cycle of birth, growth, and death.

From these premises we can draw some conclusions as to human-caused suffering; then as to what we cannot explain, and so often refer to as "acts of God."

We can hurt others—and others can hurt us. Indeed, people do hurt each other—physically and emotionally—

on purpose, carelessly, or even innocently. This is a necessary element of free choice. Rabbi Kushner puts it this way:

> In order to let us be free, in order to let us be human, God has to leave us free to choose to do right or to do wrong. If we are not free to choose evil, then we are not free to *choose* good either. Like the animals, we can only be convenient or inconvenient, obedient or disobedient. We can no longer be moral, which means we can no longer be human. . . .
>
> Why, then, do bad things happen to good people? One reason is that our being human leaves us free to hurt each other, and God can't stop us without taking away the freedom that makes us human. . . .[1]

Without the possibility of injury, we could not have freedom in our use of the laws of nature. For example, did you ever drop something which fell and was broken by the fall? It wasn't the fault of gravity,—which is always present, and about which you surely knew. Maybe it was your own clumsiness. But our freedom to use the laws of nature includes the possibility of injury as well as benefits. Without gravity, the planets and stars would spin out of control and maybe crash into each other. Without gravity we would need to tie ourselves down, or else sail off into space. So maybe we should agree that the laws of nature are for our benefit and it is only when we are clumsy or when we misuse these laws that harm results to ourselves or others.

We also hurt ourselves in various ways. We eat too much, or eat the wrong kinds of foods; and poor diet causes some diseases. We become "couch potatoes" even though we know full well that lack of exercise contributes to heart disease. We succumb to materialism, overspend, pile up debt, and end up bankrupt. We get into the driver's seat of an automobile after having had "a couple of beers" and run over a pedestrian or hit another car. Penalties may be administered by man's legal system for violation of society's laws; and the resultant suffering may well involve people other than the offender himself, such as his family or his creditors or his friends. These are only a few of the unwise conscious actions we take, although we know better; and by them we victimize ourselves. Other examples of people injuring themselves and other people can be multiplied; but the point is already made.

All of this is man-caused suffering, i.e., the direct result of an act of some human being, or his failure to act when he could and should have acted. All of these consequences are avoidable. So we must agree that harm and suffering often come to man by other man, not by act of God.

What we have said so far follows from reason and common sense. Now, assuming the existence of God, let us ask ourselves whether we can find reasons for suffering that are consistent with a loving Creator? If we can accept one or more explanations, the fact that we cannot understand *all* suffering and pain does not disprove God any more than the inability of science to fully explain the origin of life disproves life. Even expert theologians admit:

> . . . Answers to the problem of innocent suffering vary, indicating their inadequacy . . .[2]

In this exercise we can turn to the Bible, which tells us something as to the reasons for human suffering.

- Suffering may be the natural result of sin.[3] This is to say that either active disobedience of God's moral law or simply the failure to avail oneself of the opportunity to do what is right may cause suffering for oneself or for others.[4] Again, this is suffering caused by people, not by God.

- Suffering may be God's chastening for sin, even if it does not appear to be the natural and immediate result.[5] Still, the punishment is brought on by man himself.
- Suffering may be so that God's mercy and mighty works might be seen, such as by Jesus giving sight to the blind man.[6] Healing the distress of one may benefit many.
- We may have to endure drought to show us that the rain *will* come, so we can practice patience with faith that God will provide. Likewise, floods may come so that we will be grateful for the rainbow. So some suffering may be to test one's faith, an opportunity that character may be enhanced by steadfastness in trial.[7] Most of us have seen cases where people are better for having been through trying times. Character is built in adversity; seldom in affluence.
- Suffering may enable one to serve as an example for others.[8]
- Suffering provides the opportunity for us to serve one another. As long as we are self-centered, we think only of those troubles that affect ourselves and give little attention to those which affect other people. Could it be that a God of love lets trouble come to others so that we may have the opportunity to serve; or vice versa, that our hurting gives someone else the chance to help? Wouldn't life be sad if the only opportunities for service were in commercial ventures or politics? Suffering is a teacher of many things and it teaches us to recognize the hurt in others, to sympathize, and to help. The spirit

of service is born of suffering. It leads us to look out-side ourselves to meet the needs of others with com-passion and charity. It affords us the opportunity to obey Jesus' command "that ye love one another."⁹

- Suffering motivates us to look for its causes, so as to develop methods to prevent its recurrence. To this end, research in medicine has been funded through philanthropy and pursued by scientists dedicated to finding ways to prevent or cure diseases.
- Suffering leads us to count our blessings when we see—always—somebody worse off than we ourselves.
- Likewise, suffering may be so that one who produces the "fruit" of the Spirit by influence on others is "pruned" in order to bear more fruit.¹⁰

Indeed, when viewed from the proper perspective, we can see that God doesn't always *cause* distress. Furthermore, God's action can be *curative* in discipline, in charity and in leading man to depend on God.

Look around and see people who have suffered from disease, tragedy, or the actions of other people. How many of them have turned to God for help in dealing with their problem? How many of them will tell you that without his support they would have never made it through? Our own experience and that of others whom we see in trouble give us assurance to trust God.¹¹

This effort to deal with the issues of innocent and un-explainable suffering is the subject matter of the Old Testa-ment book of Job. Job is a good and wealthy man who, suddenly and without any apparent explanation, loses his wealth and his children. Three friends come to visit with him. They believe that God favors the good people with wealth and children but punishes the wicked with depriva-tion of both. Therefore they call upon Job to confess his

hidden sins. Job protests that he has not sinned and, consequently, cannot understand why he now suffers with poverty, the loss of his children, and even painful and unsightly boils all over his body. He complains that injustice is being done to him and cries out to God for a hearing.

Again we look to Rabbi Kushner for some insight. Speaking of Job's friends, he wrote:

> . . . They believe, and want to continue believing, in God's goodness and power. But if Job is innocent, then God must be guilty—guilty of making an innocent man suffer. With that at stake, they find it easier to stop believing in *Job's* goodness than to stop believing in God's perfection. . . .
>
> We see this psychology at work elsewhere, blaming the victim so that evil doesn't seem quite so irrational and threatening, . . . Blaming the victim is a way of reassuring ourselves that the world is not as bad a place as it may seem, and that there are good reasons for people's suffering. It helps fortunate people believe that their good fortune is deserved, rather than being a matter of luck. It makes everyone feel better—except the victim, who now suffers the double abuse of social condemnation on top of his original misfortune. . . .[12]

But God didn't blame Job. While we have seen that the victim is often to blame, it is not always so. Rabbi Kushner explains by saying that some things happen for no reason, that there is randomness in the universe.[13] I don't read the book of Job to warrant the conclusion that Job's suffering resulted from some random cause or causes, even though it seems clear that God was not willing to give an explanation to Job.

God spoke to Job "out of the whirlwind" and asked him:

Where were you when I laid the foundation of the earth?[14]

Have you ever in your life commanded the morning,
and caused the dawn to know its place;[15]

Where is the way to the dwelling of light? And darkness, where is its place?[16]

Can you bind the chains of the Pleiades, or loose the
cords of Orion?[17]

Who has put wisdom in the innermost being, or has
given understanding to the mind?[18]

Is it by your understanding that the hawk soars, stretch-
ing his wings toward the south? Is it at your command
that the eagle mounts up, and makes his nest on high?[19]

Job understood. Not that he understood why he had
suffered, but he understood his presumption in question-
ing God, whom he should trust even when he cannot understand the reasons for his suffering and is innocent of
any wrongdoing.

George MacDonald has written:

> . . . In this world power is no *proof* of righteousness; but
> was it likely that he who could create should be unrigh-
> teous? . . . Did he (Job) understand his own being, his-
> tory, and destiny? Should not God's ways in these also
> be beyond his understanding? Might he not trust him to
> do him justice? In such high affairs as the rights of a live
> soul, might not matters be involved too high for Job?
> The maker of Job was so much greater than Job, that his
> ways with him might well be beyond his comprehen-
> sion! God's thoughts were higher than his thoughts, as
> the heavens were higher than the earth!

The true child, the righteous man, will trust absolutely, against all appearances, the God who has created in him the love of righteousness.

God does not, I say, tell Job why he had afflicted him: he rouses his child-heart to trust.. . . [20]

Man's question as to the cause of unexplained suffering proceeds from the very sense of right and wrong which was instilled in man by the righteous God. And shall man then accuse the righteous God of unrighteousness? So MacDonald says, "While the Lord liveth, we need not fear."[21] Job has taught us to trust in God.

In reading this poem, we have the advantage over Job. From the beginning we are told that Job "was blameless, upright, fearing God, and turning away from evil"[22] and that his suffering came because God let Satan test Job.[23] And, of course, suffering may come from Satan.[24] But the lesson for us is the same as that for Job. Given our relationship to a loving, omnipotent God, we are to trust him and his promises to be with us in times of tribulation. So we can say with Paul:

Who shall separate us from the love of Christ? Shall tribulation, or stress, or persecution, or famine, or nakedness, or peril, or sword? Just as it is written, "for Thy sake we are being put to death all day long; we were considered as sheep to be slaughtered". But in all these things we overwhelmingly conquer through Him who loved us. For I am convinced that neither death, nor life, nor angels, nor principalities, nor things present, nor things to come, nor powers, nor height, nor depth, nor any other created thing, shall be able to separate us from the love of God, which is in Christ Jesus our Lord.[25]

Again in his letter to the Romans, Paul speaks of tribulations, saying:

> ... but we glory in tribulations also; knowing that tribulation worketh patience; and patience, experience; and experience, hope; and hope maketh not ashamed; because the love of God is shed abroad in our hearts by the Holy Ghost which is given unto us.[26]

We conclude that human suffering does not either indict God or disprove his existence. To the contrary, we see many ways in which mankind benefits in the ultimate result of pain; and we can recognize the loving hand of God, even as did Job and Paul.

The next question is whether we might properly pray that God not only give us courage and strength to bear affliction, but that he intervene to prevent or terminate our suffering. The answer was given to us in Gethsemene when Jesus prayed that there might be another course, but then submitted himself to the cross notwithstanding his human trepidation, so that God's will would be done.

We must realize that God does not always intervene to prevent suffering. Examples and reasons abound. If he were to always intervene, man's free will would be negated and there would be neither merit in obedience nor consequences to sin. Moreover, we could not depend upon nature's laws for their good effects if they were suspended to avoid pain. So miracles occur only when God has a purpose in them. Thus the prayer: "Thy will be done." And sometimes he turns away. Jesus' cry on the cross, "My God, my God, why hast thou forsaken me," calls to our minds a weeping Father averting his sight from a Son being crucified to accomplish the Father's will: salvation of those who believe.

We must remember that God's way often looks upside down from the perspective of mankind. Few, if any, of us would say—

- Blessed are they which are persecuted for righteousness sake,[27]
- Blessed are ye, when men shall revile you, and persecute you and shall say all manner of evil against you falsely, for my sake,[28]
- Lay not up for yourselves treasures upon earth,[29]
- Love your enemies, bless them that curse you, do good to them that hate you, and pray for them which despitefully use you, and persecute you,[30] and
- A man's foes shall be they of his own household.[31]

But these and other values like them are exactly what Jesus taught. So the death of a young person in what appears to be a senseless act to us may make some sense to God. God's purpose for some lives may be met early on and in tragedy, as a lesson for others.

Yet, even the things which we view as wrongs perpetrated by others against us, God can change to good and beneficial. We remember Paul's assurance to the Romans:

> And we know that God causes all things to work together for good to those who love God, to those who are called according to His purpose.[32]

Therefore, with Job we can trust God even when we don't understand.

And miracles do happen when God has a purpose in them,—such as to glorify himself. God intervenes through means which appear to be natural—through men or medicines or other mundane methods.

THE BRIDGE OF FAITH

What hands has God on earth to use but ours?
What feet has he to send but ours?

So his intervention is seen by materialists to be nothing more than coincidence, and only those who through faith "see" the spiritual can recognize that prayer changes things. Dr. Siegel says, "Coincidence is God's way of remaining anonymous."[33]

CHAPTER FOUR

SIN: ITS SEED, ITS GARDEN AND ITS FRUIT

Nowadays it is quite out of fashion to speak of sin. Sin is an ugly word. Nobody likes to hear it said. Nobody likes to read about it. But truth requires its use, and truth cannot have it "sugar-coated." To shrink from the use of this ugly word would itself be deceptive and, therefore, sinful.

Don't tune this out or turn the page too quickly because you don't need *me* preaching to *you*. Let's get two things straight:

- *I'm* a sinner, and
- *You're* a sinner, too.

The Bible is clear about this.

For *all* have sinned, and come short of the glory of God.[1]

If we say that we have no sin, we deceive ourselves, and the truth is not in us.[2]

So we are *two sinners* talking to each other; or, more accurately, because I got here first and wrote it down: one sinner talking to another, certainly no worse than himself, and likely not much better. The issue is not whether you and I are sinners. The issue is how to recognize sin and deal with it.

Pop psychologists and social scientists pander to society's search for somebody else to blame for every wrongdoer. These "experts" usually divide the blame between the perpetrator's parents and his victim. Sometimes they blame "the culture." The evildoer himself is encouraged to have no guilt, because of his hidden childhood abuse or his suppressed feelings about being lonely or rejected.[3] This prevalent societal attitude is diametrically contrary to biblical teachings concerning sin and the sinner's responsibility for it.

In fairness, not all are willing to summarily dismiss sin. Twenty-five years ago, one of the great American psychiatrists, Dr. Karl Menninger, wrote:

> ... There *is* immorality; there *is* unethical behavior; there *is* wrongdoing. And I hope to show that there is usefulness in retaining the concept, and indeed the word, SIN, which now shows some signs of returning to public acceptance. I would like to help this trend along.[4]

> ... I have pursued the possible usefulness of reviving the use of the word "sin"—not for the word's sake, but for the reintroduction of the concepts of guilt and moral responsibility.[5]

Unfortunately, things may be even worse since his death.

Christian evangelism's invitation to accept God's forgiveness presupposes guilt because, without guilt there would be no need for forgiveness. Consequently, the unbelieving world apart from Christianity, through the media, entertainment, and its other voices goes on the attack. At every hand it screams at Christians who express concerns about community and family values, claiming that "religion" has no business in the public arena and must not "force" religious values on other people. This is usually done under the cloak of the Constitution, in the name of "freedom," or by misinterpretation of the rubric "separation of church and state."

Whatever their method of escapism or denial, all who profess to believe in God must someday face up to the fact of sin.

Sin is the antithesis of God.

God is truth. Sin is falsehood and deceit. God is love. Sin is rancor and hatred. God is righteousness. Sin is unrighteousness. God urges patience. Sin wants immediate gratification. God is justice. Sin is oppression. God is kind. Sin is mean. Just as we cannot fully describe the goodness of God, we cannot fully describe the evils of sin.

While God has a specific purpose for each of us, in general terms his will and purpose for the life of every man, woman and child is to serve as his hands on earth, in imitation of Christ. Every departure, whether in attitude or act, from that purpose is sin. Every distraction from that purpose is temptation.

So we have some hard lessons. If we concede that distractions from what the Apostle Paul calls "a more excellent way" tempt us to sin, we need to ask "what distractions?" Surprisingly, we learn that even the most precious of our relationships, those of family, can provide the distractions which lead us astray. So Jesus said:

> If any man come to me, and hate not his father, and mother, and wife, and children, and brethren, and sisters, yea, and his own life also, he cannot be my disciple.[6]

And the Gospel according to Matthew tells us:

> While he yet talked to the people, behold, his mother
> and his brethren stood without, desiring to speak with
> him. Then one said unto him, Behold, thy mother and
> thy brethren stand without, desiring to speak with thee.
> But he answered and said unto him that told him, Who
> is my mother? And who are my brethren? And he
> stretched forth his hand toward his disciples, and said,
> Behold my mother and my brethren! For whosoever shall
> do the will of my Father which is in heaven, the same is
> my brother, and sister, and mother.[7]

This is not to deny family responsibilities, about which the
Bible has much to speak from beginning to end. However,
it suggests that sometimes our children are but extensions
of ourselves, and get in the way of our service to God. It is
to say that, even more important than family relationships,
responsibilities and values, are the claims of God on each
life. And family is but one of our distractions, of which
there are many.

According to Alister E. McGrath, the Old Testament
concept of righteousness is a "personal concept" stemming
from the "demands and obligations of a relationship between two persons." So he writes:

> . . . Just as "righteousness" is primarily concerned with
> faithfulness, so "sin" is primarily concerned with faith-
> lessness. While the biblical concept of sin has many as-
> pects that could rightly be described as forensic or legal
> (such as the ideas of "missing the mark" or "falling short
> of what is required"), the idea of the betrayal of a per-
> sonal relationship is fundamental to a biblical understand-
> ing of sin. Sin is about failing to trust God, challenging
> His authority, or failing to take His promises seriously

(see Ps. 106: 24–27)—in short, a failure to trust in God.
. . . [8]

Others look at the Greek words which are translated as "sin" in the New Testament and use terms like "to miss the mark," "injustice," "unrighteousness," "to be without the law" or "lawlessness."[9] Ted Peters goes on to write:

> At the heart or essence of all sin is the failure to trust God. Sin is our unwillingness to acknowledge our creatureliness and dependence upon the God of grace. We pursue sin in the illusory and vain effort to establish our own lives on an independent and secure basis. The effect of such sin is evil in the form of insensitivity, uncaringness, injustice, cruelty, and destruction aimed at our fellow creatures in this world. In short, sin is the failure to live up to Jesus' commandments to love God and love neighbor.[10]

Another respected theologian recently defined sin as "any failure to conform to the moral law of God in act, attitude, or nature".[11]

Augustine taught that man has free will but is sinful by nature, as if bias to sin were an inherited trait. Pelagius taught that man is free by nature and may choose to be either good or evil. Both held that man is responsible for his choices and will ultimately face a day of reckoning. Writing in the early fifth century, both of them were familiar with the Bible, but their perspectives differed. Pelagius saw the lawless behavior of Christians in Rome; and his point of view led him to lay down the requirements of a rigidly moralistic religion, which was renounced by the Church because it was thought to make salvation depend on works. Even so, Pelagianism reappears in every generation under some guise or other. On the other hand, Augustine himself had gone through experiences recounted in his *Confessions*,[12] which led him to believe that man's only hope for salvation lay in the grace of God. Their issue was whether salvation was by grace or by works, but their views reflected their differences about sin.[13]

Since the Genesis story of the "forbidden fruit" and the fall of man, men have thought of sin as being caused by Satan, "the evil one." No doubt *temptation* often comes from Satan. Sin is usually a product of self-centeredness, to which temptation comes easily.

We too often treat our selves and our things as more important than God. Our selves and our things become our gods, and we become even more and more self-centered. In so speaking of self-centeredness, I don't mean to imply criticism of self-confidence, self-control, and self-respect. These are all good qualities, if not taken too far. Self-confidence comes from having tried and succeeded. Self-control is essential to a morally upright life. Self-respect comes from living up to high moral and spiritual standards.

"Self-esteem" is too often equated with a love of self, and it is an anaesthetic for sin. The "feel good about yourself" philosophy denies the reality of sin, and it makes an easy victim for temptation. Indeed it is the self-centeredness in each of us that focuses attention on our selves instead of on God and others. It is impossible to obey Jesus' commandments to love God and neighbor if our focus is on our selves.[14]

Self-centeredness produces lust, which is another way of describing the desire for immediate gratification of one's appetites, and without regard for other people. Self-centeredness leads to envy of others whose position or possessions are attractive, and to covetousness in the desire for such position or possessions. When coupled with the

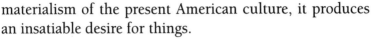

materialism of the present American culture, it produces an insatiable desire for things.

Speaking of the "eight deadly sins", the author says parenthetically:

> . . . There were eight in the original list drawn up in the Egyptian desert about 390 (A.D.): vanity, arrogance, melancholy, accidie (torpor and indifference), covetousness, lust, gluttony and anger. The later list of seven drawn up by Pope Gregory about 600 (A.D.) fused the first two into "pride" and the next two into "sloth", and added envy.[15]

Peters writes of a later time:

> . . . The medievals listed seven serious or deadly vices that they said violated both natural reason and divine law: pride, envy, anger, covetousness, sadness, gluttony, and lust. It is worth noting that this list of seven does not include any actions or deeds. It is a septenary of habits or dispositions or character traits that influence our actions or deeds.[16]

We can easily see that these attitudes and traits proceed from self-centeredness. These sinful character traits might well be contrasted with the four "cardinal" virtues: prudence, justice, fortitude, and temperance, as well as with the three "theological" virtues: faith, hope and love.

From self-centeredness comes pride. It is the contrary of humility, which is born of the proper relationship between man and God. C. S. Lewis describes pride with his usual insight and imagery.

> . . . There is one vice of which no man in the world is free; which every one in the world loathes when he

sees it in someone else; and of which hardly any people, except Christians, ever imagine that they are guilty themselves. . . .

The vice I am talking of is Pride. . . . According to Christian teachers, the essential vice, the utmost evil, is Pride. . . . Pride leads to every other vice: it is the complete anti-God state of mind.

. . . The point is that each person's pride is in competition with every one else's pride. . . . Now what you want to get clear is that Pride is *essentially* competitive—is competitive by its very nature—while the other vices are competitive only, so to speak, by accident. Pride gets no pleasure out of having something, only out of having more of it than the next man. . . .

The Christians are right: it is Pride which has been the chief cause of misery in every nation and every family since the world began. Other vices may sometimes bring people together: you may find good fellowship and jokes and friendliness among drunken people or unchaste people. But Pride always means enmity,—it *is* enmity. And not only enmity between man and man, but enmity to God.[17]

Pride and self-centeredness are joined at the hip. Through the focus on self and via pride, we *take* the glory instead of *giving* the glory to God. Pride also gets in the way of forgiveness; and our refusal to forgive is the scariest of sins because it gets in the way of God's forgiving us. Jesus taught "the Lord's Prayer" and then said:

But if ye forgive not men their trespasses, neither will your Father forgive your trespasses.[18]

We must think of this, instead of just rattling off the Lord's Prayer as if it were the alphabet or the numbers from one to ten.

And pride is not the only indicia of self-centeredness. To the contrary, every attitude or vice mentioned by Pope Gregory or the midievals, or listed today by the Roman Catholic catechism,[19] is traced to self-centeredness.

So sin itself, not some particular sinful attitude or specific sinful act, but sin in the aggregate, in the whole, is rebellion of the creature against its Creator. It is setting up one's self as god, in place of the one true God. Oswald Chambers has it this way:

> . . . The disposition of sin is not immorality and wrongdoing, but the disposition of self-realization—I am my own god. This disposition may work out in decorous morality or in indecorous immorality, but it has the one basis, my claim to my right to my self. When Our Lord faced men with all the forces of evil in them, and men who were clean living and moral and upright, He did not pay any attention to the moral degradation of the one or to the moral attainment of the other; He looked at something we do not see, viz., the disposition.[20]

A highly respected Baptist pastor puts it this way:

> . . . The most likely theory as to the origin of sin is that it is due to man's being a free intelligent being with the power of choice. This theory agrees with our knowledge of man, God, and the Bible. Sin, therefore, is in the will before it is in the act.

> The biblical account of the origin of sin is found in Genesis 3:1–7. There man's free choice was confronted with

God's will and Satan's will. The will of man obeyed Satan and disobeyed God. Hence the transgression. . . . [21]

Perhaps with this in mind we can come down somewhere between Augustine and Pelagius and simply agree that, when blessed with free will by his Creator, man used that free will to claim his life for himself and, thereby, became self-centered and disposed to an attitude of sin. As Jesus says, we are slaves of sin.[22] Quoting St. Augustine, the catechism says that:

> . . . Sin is thus "love of oneself even to contempt of God."[23]

Before we consider the fruit of sin,—its specifics and its consequences—we might well conclude that temptation is the seed of sin and comes from outside the self, but finds fertile ground in the self so that sin grows like weeds in a garden. The weeds of sin choke out the flowers and vegetables because the gardener chooses to tend the weeds instead of the flowers or vegetables. So the garden, i.e., the life, becomes overgrown with weeds and bears the bitter fruit of sin.

The fruit of sin should be considered both in sin's active aspect and in its failures—in both its assertive and negative configurations.

Active sins are acts of rebellion against God, the conscious disobedience of moral and religious values. For example, they proceed from one or more of the "cardinal sins" in specific acts. The sinful attitudes bear fruit in actions. Active sins include theft or other misuse or destruction of the property of others. Other examples are lies, including fraud, deception and half-truth. At its worst, perhaps, a sinful attitude produces murder which, by specific intent, is meant to frustrate the purpose of God for another person's life.

Sin in its passive side is the failure to take advantage of opportunities to serve God's purpose or to do his will. This may be even more serious than sin in its active character. We can foresee its punishment at the Judgment Day when, Jesus said, the sheep are divided from the goats. Those who have everlasting life are those "sheep" who met the needs of the hungry, the thirsty, the stranger, and the sick.[24] Those "goats" who ignored their opportunities to express God's love for others by feeding the hungry, clothing the naked, and visiting the sick are to be sent "away into everlasting punishment."[25]

"If only . . .". The saddest words are "what might have been". Sometimes the greatest cost is that of opportunity lost. Examples abound.

- A church without a leader in a potentially productive area.
- "Someday I am going to write a book—or read one".
- The wealthy man who wishes he could find a charity "worthy" of his support.
- "I wish I had told my uncle how much he meant to me—before he died."

Big things. Little things. Even a kind word left unspoken. Opportunities missed.

We have looked at sin in its relationship to God and to other people. We must look at its connection with "things," with material possessions. Are automobiles or houses or clothing or food or other "things" wrong? No, of course not. These things are all amoral. That means that, in and of themselves, they are neither moral nor immoral. They are simply things. The issue is how they are used.

Too much food is gluttony, and that is wrong. Too scanty clothing is tempting to others, and to tempt others is wrong. Houses may be used for evil purposes such as "crack houses," as well as for good, such as to raise a family. Automobiles can be driven recklessly; or they may be used to travel to church.

So it is the user and his motivation, not the thing itself, which determines whether or not use of the thing is sinful. This becomes a matter of special importance in a materialistic culture such as we see in America today. We encounter questions such as "Are riches some evidence of God's payment for being good? Is poverty God's punishment for being bad?" Jesus clearly answers both questions "No." Following his encounter with the rich young ruler, Jesus said to his disciples:

> . . . how hard is it for them that trust in riches to enter into the kingdom of God![26]

Elsewhere he said:

> But woe unto you that are rich! For ye *have received* your consolation.[27]

But he blessed the poor.[28]

So, contrary to the general view, we might well commiserate with the rich. They have an enormous burden of stewardship; not just in tithing or supporting a religious institution, but in making appropriate use of the material assets entrusted to their care. We remember Jesus having said:

> . . . For unto whomsoever much is given, of him shall be much required: and to whom men have committed much, of him they will ask the more.[29]

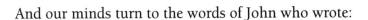

And our minds turn to the words of John who wrote:

> How does God's love abide in anyone who has the world's goods and sees a brother or sister in need and yet refuses help?[30]

So why all the concern about sin? Why not let people alone? The answer is three-fold:

- Sin has consequences for the sinner, consequences in the here and now;
- Sin has consequences for others,—in your life, in mine, and in the community; and
- Sin has consequences in the hereafter, about which more will be said in Chapter 5.

The present consequences or fruit of sin include frustration, guilt, lost opportunities for love and peace of mind, and enslavement. These are bitter fruits, but they follow sin as surely as the night follows day. Sadly, there are present-day consequences for people other than the sinner himself and, indeed, often times for his whole community. For examples: his lies cause others to stumble, his theft impoverishes others, and his lust produces illegitimate children who must be supported by his community through welfare. In countless other ways his sins adversely affect others than himself. Finally, of course, comes accountability. "The wages of sin is death"[31] and "it is appointed for men to die once and after this comes judgment".[32]

The fruits of sin have given rise to the need for law, charity and evangelism. In law is an effort to protect the sinners' victims and the community. In charity is the effort to help the victims cope with the consequences of the sins of others. In evangelism is the purpose of persuading sinners to avoid the eternal consequences of judgment.

One cannot leave this subject matter without an exhortation to make use of the best way to avoid sin. Flee temptation. Stay away from places where temptations lie in wait. Flee temptation. Avoid people who are not afraid of "the tempter's snare." Flee temptation.

The Apostle Paul wrote:

> There hath no temptation taken you but such as is common to man; but God is faithful, who will not suffer you to be tempted above that ye are able; but will with the temptation also make a way to escape, that ye may be able to bear it.[33]

So we conclude that there could be lawlessness without God, were there the laws of a society to be broken. But there would be no sin without God, because it is the substitution for God of self-centeredness which prepares the disposition or attitude for sin. There could be no sin without God because sin is best defined as everything which God is not. Sin is the contrariety of our Creator.

CHAPTER FIVE

HELLFIRE AND DAMNATION

In the not-too-distant past, evangelists called their listeners to the altar by preaching "hellfire and damnation." That is not a popular sermon subject these days. Indeed, there are many who deeply resent any suggestion that their eternal destination may be hell.

As early as the Reformation there began what has been called "a long Protestant doubt about hell".[1]

> ... Then the West lost interest in it. With the decline of the moral importance of hell as a place of punishment, people stopped making pictures of the descent into hell. The phrase in the creed became a relic, a poetic assertion of the solidarity of Jesus with all the dead, no longer needed as proof of the justice of God.[2]

But not one jot nor tittle has been erased from the Bible; and the Bible speaks explicitly of hell. No matter the modern mind, the subject of hellfire and damnation is still biblical.

The word "hell" is used in the Old Testament to translate a Hebrew word *sheol*, which means the underworld, or place of the departed dead. In the New Testament, the Greek word *hades* is used to mean the same as *sheol*. But another Greek word *gehenna* is translated as "hell" and it is used to mean the place of punishment. Bearing the latter in mind, consider what Jesus said:

> You have heard that the ancients were told, "you shall not commit murder" and "whoever commits murder shall be liable to the court". But I say to you that everyone who is angry with his brother shall be guilty before the court; and whoever shall say to his brother, "raca"[3] shall be guilty before the supreme court; and whoever shall say, "you fool", shall be guilty enough to go into the fiery hell.[4]

> And if your right eye makes you stumble, tear it out, and throw it from you; for it is better for you that one of the parts of your body perish, than for your whole body to be thrown into hell.

> And if your right hand makes you stumble, cut it off, and throw it from you; for it is better for you that one of the parts of your body perish, than for your whole body to go into hell.[5]

> And I say to you, My friends, do not be afraid of those who kill the body, and after that have no more that they can do. But I will warn you whom to fear: fear the One who after He has killed has authority to cast into hell; yes, I tell you, fear Him![6]

Later, speaking to the scribes and Pharisees, Jesus said:

You serpents, you brood of vipers, how shall you escape the sentence of hell?[7]

The Bible also describes this place of punishment, to which it refers as "hell," in terms of fire. John the Baptist calls it "unquenchable fire."[8] Jesus echoes John the Baptist, in parabolic terms, when he warns that false prophets can be compared to trees which bear bad fruit, and then says:

Every tree that does not bear good fruit is cut down and thrown into the fire.[9]

Again, in explaining to his disciples the parable of the tares, Jesus said:

So it will be at the end of the age; the angels shall come forth, and take out the wicked from among the righteous, and will cast them into the furnace of fire; there shall be weeping and gnashing of teeth. [10]

According to Mark, Jesus said:

And if your hand causes you to stumble, cut it off; it is better for you to enter life crippled, than having your two hands, to go into hell, into the unquenchable fire.[11]

So also in the Revelation, a "lake of fire" or a "lake of fire and brimstone" is referred to as the second death, and the destiny of those whose names are not found written in "the book of life." They are described as "the cowardly and unbelieving and abominable and murderers and immoral persons and sorcerers and idolaters and all liars".[12]

The scriptures may use metaphor, allegory and analogy to make the point, but the substance is clear if the details are not. Speaking of the righteous judgment of God, and his "vengeance upon those who do not know God and upon those who do not obey the gospel of our Lord Jesus," Paul says:

> They shall suffer the punishment of eternal destruction and exclusion from the presence of the Lord and from the glory of his might, . . . [13]

God is light, love, truth, peace, and grace. If hell is exclusion from the presence of God, then it is an eternity in darkness, in lonely selfishness, without love or kindness, with nobody to trust, beset with anxiety and guilt. The conditions of hell are the antitheses of God.

Heaven will be peopled with those who have given up their egocentricity, and denied selves to be born of the Spirit. They will partake of the fruits of the Spirit which include love, joy, peace, and goodness.[14] On the other hand, those who spend their eternity in hell will spend it with others like themselves, who reject the Spirit of God and look only to their own selfish interests; those who damn others and the needs of others; those who covet what belongs to others, and then lie and cheat to get it; who steal from widows and children, then hate those to whom they have done wrong. Maybe people like that deserve each other.

How can a God of love and mercy permit any creature to spend eternity in hell? It is because accountability is a necessary corollary of freedom and choice. He is a God of righteousness and justice; and it is clear that justice requires the punishment of those who are unrighteous. But God is still love, which is why choice is expanded—and a second chance is made available—so that through repentance and faith we can have forgiveness. This is the *New* Testament,

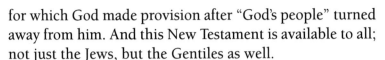

for which God made provision after "God's people" turned away from him. And this New Testament is available to all; not just the Jews, but the Gentiles as well.

Here a word about "predestination." If God is love, as the Scriptures say, how could he breath life into men whom he "pre-destined" to spend their eternity in hell? And this without a choice, without a chance, and without a hope. So there are those of us who believe that God did not pre-destine which choice any of us will make, but that God pre-destined that *all those who repent in faith will be saved.* Those who refuse to repent in faith and thereby reject God's grace and forgiveness, are left to the pre-determination that unforgiven sinners merit the hell of separation from God. There is scriptural authority for this position:

> The Lord is . . . not willing that any should perish, but that all should come to repentance.[15]

In *The Problem of Pain*, C. S. Lewis explains the morality of hell after stating the issue as follows:

> . . . Christianity, true, as always, to the complexity of the real, presents us with something knottier and more ambiguous—a God so full of mercy that He becomes man and dies by torture to avert that final ruin from His creatures, and who yet, where that heroic remedy fails, seems unwilling, or even unable, to arrest the ruin by an act of mere power. . . . And here is the real problem: so much mercy, yet still there is Hell.
>
> I am not going to try to prove the doctrine tolerable. Let us make no mistake; it is *not* tolerable. But I think the doctrine can be shown to be moral by a critique of the objections ordinarily made, or felt, against it.[16]

Lewis discusses the imagery by which "the frightful intensity of the pains of Hell" are communicated to us, and he writes:

> . . . Our Lord speaks of Hell under three symbols: first, that of punishment ("everlasting punishment", Matt. 25: 46); second, that of destruction ("fear Him who is able to destroy both body and soul in Hell," Matt. 10: 28); and thirdly, that of privation, exclusion, or banishment into "the darkness outside," as in the parables of the man without a wedding garment or of the wise and foolish virgins. The prevalent image of fire is significant because it combines the ideas of torment and destruction. Now it is quite certain that all these expressions are intended to suggest something unspeakably horrible, and any interpretation which does not face that fact is, I am afraid, out of court from the beginning. But it is not necessary to concentrate on the images of torture to the exclusion of those suggesting destruction and privation.[17]

While Calvinists may disagree, I believe that every person chooses and serves his own master—God or self—and that the service of self is sin. Think about it for a minute. Is not self-centeredness the focus of every sin?

Justice demands punishment for sin. Make no mistake, the Bible in both the Old and New Testaments clearly describes a God who will punish those who flaunt his authority and disobey his Law. The psalmist wrote:

> . . . He is coming to judge the earth; He will judge the world with righteousness, and the people with equity.[18]

Jesus also spoke of the judgment. This is what he said:

But when the Son of Man comes in His glory, and all the angels with Him, then He will sit on His glorious throne. And all the nations will be gathered before Him; and He will separate them from one another, as the shepherd separates the sheep from the goats; and He will put the sheep on His right, and the goats on the left. Then the King will say to those on His right, "Come, you who are blessed of My Father, inherit the kingdom prepared for you from the foundation of the world. . ."[19]

Then He will also say to those on His left, "Depart from Me, accursed ones, into the eternal fire which has been prepared for the devil and his angels; . . ." And these will go away into eternal punishment, but the righteous into eternal life.[20]

Who will say that Jesus lied; or that Jesus didn't know what he was talking about? Certainly not I.

But, the gospel also teaches that, out of his grace and everlasting lovingkindness, God has provided a way for sinful men to be pardoned and have eternal life in the presence of God.

In his allegory of spirits from hell taking a bus trip to the outskirts of heaven and being invited in, C. S. Lewis identifies the "teacher" whom he meets there as George MacDonald . Elsewhere Lewis has extolled MacDonald as having been continually close to the Spirit of Christ himself. In that allegory, titled *The Great Divorce*, Lewis pursues the thesis that one's eternal destiny is the consequence of one's own choice. His protagonist puts to MacDonald the issue as it is often expressed:

What some people say on earth is that the final loss of one soul gives the lie to all the joy of those who are saved.

The teacher replies:

> Son, Son, it must be one way or the other. Either the day must come when joy prevails and all the makers of misery are no longer able to infect it; or else for ever and ever the makers of misery can destroy in others the happiness they reject for themselves. I know it has a grand sound to say ye'll accept no salvation which leaves even one creature in the dark outside. But watch that sophistry or ye'll make a Dog in a Manger the tyrant of the universe.[21]

Elsewhere in the same book, MacDonald has told him:

> . . . All that are in Hell, choose it. Without that self-choice, there could be no Hell. No soul that seriously and constantly desires joy will ever miss it. Those who seek find. To those who knock it is opened.[22]

Whether one sees the "New Jerusalem" with gates of pearl and streets of gold, or not; the alternative of living with God instead of apart from him is open to our own choice. According to Jesus, each of us can choose salvation by faith, that is, by repentance and belief.

Faith is manifested by "fruit," which derives from a change of course (repentance) and a spirit of love—for God and for others. Fruit is manifested in self-denial and a life lived in accordance with God's purpose for that life. This is what is meant by the gospel where Jesus said, "If any man would come after me, let him deny himself, take up his cross daily, and follow me".[23] The cross was the purpose of Jesus' life, as he made plain in both word and deed. In speaking to Andrew and Philip about his impending crucifixion, Jesus said:

Now My soul has become troubled; and what shall I say,
"Father, save Me from this hour?" But for this purpose I
came to this hour.[24]

While none of us may see crucifixion as the purpose for his
or her own life, Jesus' crucifixion is given by him as his
purpose. So it is to be the example for us.

"Follow me," he said; and we follow him through love
of God and love of neighbors. He said, "A new commandment
I give to you, that you love one another".[25]

But what if we make mistakes? We all do. Forgiveness
is still there if we still seek it. We can look to two prime
examples, Peter and Paul. After assuring Jesus over and over
again of his love, Peter three times denied even knowing
him. Even so, he was forgiven. Paul persecuted the early
Christians. According to his own testimony, he stood by
while they stoned Stephen to death. So it was that Jesus
asked him, "Why are you persecuting Me?"[26] Yet Paul was
forgiven, by grace, and became the apostle to the Gentiles.
The examples of Peter and Paul teach us that, although we
sin, we should get up and try again.

We can likewise remember what Jesus taught about forgiveness.
Peter asked Him:

"Lord, how often shall my brother sin against me and I
forgive him? Up to seven times?" Jesus said to him, "I
do not say to you, up to seven times, but up to seventy
times seven".[27]

Now, if Jesus told Peter to forgive "up to seventy times seven,"
who can think that a God of everlasting loving-kindness will
not forgive us over and over if we truly repent and seek his
forgiveness?

In the next chapter we shall see that forgiveness is across a bridge of faith, and available to whosoever will cross under a white flag of surrender.

CHAPTER SIX

THE BRIDGE
OF FAITH

A fundamental of the Christian faith is that, by his sin, man has separated himself from God. This is because "whosoever committeth sin is the servant of sin."[1] Internally, the sinner is beset with anxiety, guilt, shame, and depression. Externally, his society must take measures to protect itself from his sin and its consequences; measures designed for retribution, deterrence, and justice. The view is dismal.

> But every man is tempted, when he is drawn away of his own lust, and enticed. Then when lust hath conceived, it bringeth forth sin: and sin, when it is finished, bringeth forth death.[2]

Moreover, death is followed by judgment. For the unrepentant sinner, that means an eternity in hell.

But, praise God! There is an alternative. God is love,[3] and what is probably the best known verse in the Bible says:

For God so loved the world, that he gave his only begotten Son, that whosoever believeth in him should not
perish, but have everlasting life.[4]

Through God's grace and our faith, we may have forgiveness of sin and the joy of salvation. So let us look at grace,
faith, forgiveness, and salvation. We shall consider all in
their context and relationship to each other.

GRACE

Out of his love proceeds God's grace. Grace is unearned
favor, freely given by God and without merit or cost on our
part. His grace first brings us to "conviction." This is the
Christian's way of describing the influence of the Holy Spirit,
which leads the sinner to recognize his sin for what it is
and to want to be rid of it. But conviction alone is not
enough. There must be some way to rid ourselves of sin, to
break its grip, to escape its guilt, and to avoid its punishment. Mere acknowledgment of sin doesn't necessarily lead
to reformation; and even reformation doesn't pay the penalty for past iniquities. The person who is convicted of sin
needs some grounds for hope.[5]

Today we are taught that we humans can solve all our
own problems, and that each of us has the right to design
his own solution. In the name of "rights," our people deny
all authority—especially the authority of a God whom they
cannot see. We have become victims of a sociopathic pop
psychology. We tend to turn anywhere but to God for help.
It is to meet man's need that, from God's grace comes his
revelation of himself and his provision for our salvation.

Philosophy may be true and good and wholesome. It
may lead to a better society if its principles are grasped and
used as a map for living with self and others. But philosophy

is not enough. It does not lead to peace on earth or to eternal life. It is only in the right relationship with God that we can look beyond philosophy—beyond reason and experience—to "see" something more, which is the life and light and love of God. It is only through God's revelation of himself that we can discern his purpose, his plan, his promise and his peace.

His grace is characteristic of God. Grace is the Creator's disposition toward humankind whom he created. Grace is kin to mercy. Both are descriptive of God's feeling toward us. Grace describes God's love for men, in his attitude and as the basis of a relationship.

Love may be one-sided and directed toward one who does not reciprocate. Those of us who love God love him because he first loved us.[6] But "God so loved the world" doesn't mean the world also loves God.[7] On the contrary, the Scriptures speak of "the world" as the enemy of God[8] — the domain of Satan.[9] Why would God love those who sin and reject him? How could God forgive Pol Pot or Adolf Hitler? For answers we look to the Bible.

An adulteress was brought to Jesus. When none cast the first stone, he said to her "Neither do I condemn thee; go, and sin no more."[10] Yet he called the religious leaders of Jerusalem "serpents" and asked them "How can ye escape the damnation of hell?"[11] Why did the Son of God see them so differently than they saw themselves? We are inclined to think that a righteous God would send all sinners to destruction. We might do just that if we were the Creator against whom his creatures rebelled, who took his name in vain—calling themselves his people and then embarrassing him by mistreating each other.

As a headnote in his book entitled *The Problem of Pain*, C. S. Lewis uses the following quotation:

THE BRIDGE OF FAITH

Love can forbear, and Love can forgive . . . but Love can never be reconciled to an unlovely object . . . He can never therefore be reconciled to your sin, because sin itself is incapable of being altered; but He may be reconciled to your person, because that may be restored.[12]

So, God can hate the sin but love the sinner; and, in grace and mercy, he can make provision for the sinner's salvation.

The Scriptures say, "by grace are ye saved"[13]. It is the "grace of God that bringeth salvation."[14] Again Paul writes, this time to the Romans:

> But now the righteousness of God has been manifested apart from the law, though testified to by the law and the prophets, the righteousness of God through faith in Jesus Christ for all who believe. . . . They are justified freely by his grace through the redemption in Christ Jesus. . . [15]

So in like manner he wrote to Titus:

> But when the kindness and generous love of God our savior appeared, not because of any righteous deeds we had done but because of his mercy, he saved us through the bath of rebirth and renewal by the Holy Spirit, whom he richly poured out on us through Jesus Christ our savior, so that we might be justified by his grace and become heirs in hope of eternal life.[16]

When the Apostle writes about justification in these letters, he is referring to God's treating the sinner as if the sinner were just or righteous. This requires grace plus forgiveness and, as elsewhere explained:

> They are *justified freely by his grace* through the redemption in Christ Jesus, whom God set forth as an expiation, *through faith*, by his blood, to prove his righteousness *because of the forgiveness of sins* previously committed, through the forbearance of God—to prove his righteousness in the present time, *that he might be righteous and justify the one who has faith in Jesus.*[17]

The righteous God has provided for our salvation by way of justification, which entails forgiveness of our sin. This is all done by his grace and through our faith.

SALVATION

The salvation of which the New Testament speaks is a salvation from the punishment of hell, but it is also salvation from potential slavery to sin here on earth. In other words, salvation is the deliverance from sin and its consequences. As Paul explained to Titus:

> For the grace of God that bringeth salvation hath appeared to all men, teaching us that, denying ungodliness and worldly lusts, we should live soberly, righteously, and godly, in this present world; looking for that blessed hope, and the glorious appearing of the great God and our Savior, Jesus Christ; who gave himself for us, that he might redeem us from all iniquity, and purify unto himself a peculiar people, zealous of good works.[18]

Speaking of Jesus' part in the provision of our salvation, Paul wrote to the Corinthians:

> For ye know the grace of our Lord Jesus Christ, that, though he was rich, yet for your sakes he became poor, that ye through his poverty might be rich.[19]

In John's Gospel we are told:

> And the Word was made flesh, and dwelt among us, (and we beheld his glory, the glory as of the only begotten of the Father,) full of grace and truth. . . .
>
> For the law was given by Moses, but grace and truth came by Jesus Christ.[20]

So also, we read in the Acts about the dispute which led to the council at Jerusalem. There, speaking of the Gentiles, Peter said:

> But we believe that through the grace of the Lord Jesus Christ we shall be saved, even as they.[21]

FAITH

On the one side is God. He is love, truth, peace, joy, and life eternal. On the other side is man. Created with free choice, he has become a self-centered sinner headed for death and hell. Between the two sides is a deep chasm. But there is a bridge—a means by which the creature can be re-linked to his Creator. That bridge is faith, and it rests upon the foundation of God's grace. Faith is the bridge between the earthly and the heavenly. Faith is the bridge between the natural and the supernatural. Faith is the bridge between the material and the spiritual. "And without faith it is impossible to please God, for whoever would approach him must believe that he exists and that he rewards those who seek him."[22]

Faith is *not* understanding. It is belief *without* understanding. Even after having followed Jesus throughout his ministry, his disciples did not understand. We read of his disciples Peter and John running to the empty tomb, where:

When Simon Peter arrived after him, he went into the tomb and saw the burial cloths there, and the cloth that had covered his head, not with the burial cloths, but rolled up in a separate place. Then the other disciple also went in, the one who had arrived at the tomb first, and *he saw and believed. For they did not yet understand* the scripture that he had to rise from the dead.[23]

Jesus had taught his disciples that they must be as little children in order to enter the kingdom of God.[24] This was to say that they must believe even those teachings of Jesus which they did not understand; as children do. After his resurrection Jesus appeared to his disciples;

And he said unto them, "These are the words which I spake unto you, while I was yet with you, that all things must be fulfilled, which were written in the law of Moses, and in the prophets, and in the psalms, concerning me." *Then opened he their understanding, that they might understand the scriptures,* and said unto them, "Thus it is written, and thus it behooved Christ to suffer, and to rise from the dead the third day: and that repentance and remission of sins should be preached in his name among all nations, beginning at Jerusalem. *And ye are witnesses of these things . . .*" [25]

The Apostle Paul, writing to the Corinthians, provides us with a marvelous explanation of this concept that faith reaches beyond man's wisdom and understanding. He wrote:

When I came to you, brothers, proclaiming the mystery of God, I did not come with sublimity of words or of wisdom. For I resolved to know nothing while I was with you except Jesus Christ, and him crucified. I came to you in weakness and fear and much trembling, and my message and my proclamation were not with persuasive words of wisdom, but with a demonstration of spirit and power, so that your faith might rest not on human wisdom but on the power of God . . .

Now the natural person does not accept what pertains to the Spirit of God, for to him it is foolishness, and he cannot understand it, because it is judged spiritually.[26]

Faith does not foreclose or even limit reason. Faith goes beyond reason. So, while Paul writes of spiritual things being "spiritually discerned,"[27] he provides throughout his epistles the rationale for Christian belief and behavior. When he wrote of the wisdom of the world being foolishness,[28] Paul meant that reason alone does not understand spiritual concepts. Reason—even abstract reason—relates to matter, the material world. Its premises are experience and observation of the physical, and it draws its conclusions in physical terms. While philosophy probes spiritual subjects, its conclusions are tested in the material and seldom utilized for more than learned papers and debate among scholars.

For *since*, in the wisdom of God, *the world did not know God through wisdom, God decided, through the foolishness of our proclamation,*[29] *to save those who believe.* For Jews demand signs and Greeks desire wisdom, but *we proclaim Christ crucified*, a stumbling block to Jews and foolishness to Gentiles, but to those who are the called, both Jews and Greeks, Christ the power of God and the wisdom of God. For God's foolishness is wiser than human wisdom, and God's weakness is stronger than human strength.[30]

And the writer to the Hebrews, in his famous "faith chapter," said:

By faith we understand that the worlds were prepared by the word of God, so that what is seen was not made out of things which are visible.[31]

Paul had been called to be a witness.[32] Jesus had said to his disciples that they were to be witnesses.[33] Peter claimed to be an eyewitness.[34] Luke heard the gospel from eyewitnesses.[35] Witnesses tell of facts which they have experienced through their senses; and conclusions are drawn from relating those facts to other knowledge or experience.

The word "witness" as used in the New Testament translates a Greek word from which is also derived our word "martyr"; so it means one who "gives testimony to the truth at the expense of his life."[36] These witnesses testified of the gospel and, as Peter put it:

. . . we have not followed cunningly devised fables, when we made known unto you the power and coming of our Lord Jesus Christ, but were eyewitnesses of his majesty. For he received from God the Father honor and glory, when there came such a voice to him from the excellent glory, "This is my beloved Son, in whom I am well pleased." And this voice which came from heaven we heard, when we were with him in the holy mount.[37]

Likewise, John wrote about that "which we have heard, which we have seen with our eyes, which we have looked upon, and our hands have handled, of the Word of life . . . that which we have seen and heard."[38]

Based on the testimony of these witnesses, we can reasonably believe the gospel.

So across the bridge of faith we can be drawn to God through Christ.

And faith has an object. The object of man's faith is God. It is not only that we believe; it is that we believe in God. This belief in God motivates us to trust and obey. This is the faith that works.

Here is a word of caution. Faith is not as simple or as easy as sometimes we hear it described. A sinner who feels guilt, shame, and remorse when convicted must not be misled by emotional pleas and music. Crossing the bridge of faith requires complete surrender. Julius Caesar crossed the Rubicon to do battle. A sinner who crosses the bridge of faith must do so under a white flag of surrender, offering his life to serve a new Lord and Master.[39]

Faith comes in a package. That is to say that faith includes or is accompanied by these essential elements:

- Repentance,[40] which means turning away from sin to God;
- Trust,[41] in the promises of God and in Jesus, "the mediator of the new covenant,"[42] by which the Father promises everlasting life to those who believe in the Son;[43]
- Obedience,[44] which follows from the changed relationship between the believer and God; and
- Changed lives, shown by love[45] and service.[46]

Each of us has a choice for life. I can choose to serve myself and thereby become the slave to sin. Or I can choose to become the servant of God. After leading the children of Israel into Canaan, Joshua spoke to them shortly before his death. He told them:

. . . choose for yourselves today whom you will serve.
. . . but as for me and my house, we will serve the Lord.[47]

It is a lifetime choice, lived and renewed day by day. By and through the Holy Spirit, it grows in sanctification, a theological word meaning "set apart" and a concept somewhat difficult to comprehend.[48]

This choice calls for obedience,—even without understanding—"as a little child." A child is to obey its parents even if the only explanation he receives is "because I say so."[49] So faith requires obedience—understanding or not. Remember the old gospel song: "Trust and Obey"?

Saving faith comes by God's grace but it produces such works that James could write:

> What use is it, my brethren, if a man says he has faith, but he has no works? Can that faith save him? If a brother or sister is without clothing and in need of daily food, and one of you says to them, "go in peace, be warmed and be filled," and yet you do not give them what is necessary for their body, what use is that? Even so faith, if it has no works, is dead, being by itself. But someone may well say "you have faith, and I have works; show me your faith without the works, and I will show you my faith by my works."[50]

These works are produced by obedience to Jesus' commandment "that ye love one another, as I have loved you."[51] As believers, we are the body of Christ.[52] So we are his hands on earth by which he can answer prayer. Thus the "vine" of which he spoke to his disciples can bear fruit.[53]

Faith is a bridge, the foundation of which is God's grace. Use it. Don't try to cross the chasm from self-centeredness and sin to God and salvation on a bridge that you yourself build or one designed by philosophy or one constructed out of "things" or "works" or one pointed out to you by false prophets. Only the bridge of faith is sufficient. This bridge of faith may seem rickety at first—but try it and you will feel its strength.[54] It may seem long, with the other end out of sight, but believe and persevere.

FORGIVENESS

The bridge of faith leads to forgiveness. We read much in the Old Testament about forgiveness. Joseph forgave his brothers, even though they had sold him into slavery in Egypt.[55] Moses asked God to forgive the people of Israel for making and worshiping a golden calf.[56] He even offered himself as an atonement for their sin.[57] Psalms 25 and 86 are two of David's prayers for forgiveness. At the dedication of the temple, Solomon asked God to forgive the people when they prayed facing the temple;[58] and God agreed to do so.[59] God told Jeremiah of the new covenant to come, saying "I will forgive their iniquity, and I will remember their sin no more."[60] While the Jews were in captivity, Daniel prayed for God's forgiveness and the restoration of Jerusalem.[61] His prayer was answered.

The new covenant came with Jesus, who brought the revelation of God and forgiveness through his atoning death on the cross. We read in Luke of a sinful woman who learned that Jesus was having dinner at the home of a Pharisee. She "brought an alabaster box of ointment" and, as Jesus reclined at the dinner table in the fashion of those days, she:

> . . . stood at his feet behind him weeping, and began to wash his feet with tears, and did wipe them with the

hairs of her head, and kissed his feet, and anointed them with the ointment.[62]

The Pharisee was critical because Jesus let the sinful woman touch him. Jesus knew his critical thoughts. So he told a parable of forgiveness, then compared her kindness to the host's limited hospitality. Jesus spoke further, saying:

> ". . . Wherefore I say unto thee, her sins, which are many, are forgiven; . . ." And he said unto her, "Thy sins are forgiven". And they that sat at meat with him began to say within themselves, "Who is this that forgiveth sins also?" And he said to the woman, "Thy faith hath saved thee; go in peace".[63]

So we learn that the woman, whose sins were many, received through Jesus forgiveness and salvation because of her faith.

The New Testament writers speak often of forgiveness. For example, John says:

> If we confess our sins, he is faithful and just to forgive us our sins, and to cleanse us from all unrighteousness.[64]

> I write unto you, little children, because your sins are forgiven for his name's sake.[65]

When they were brought before the council and reminded by the High Priest that the council had commanded them to not teach in the name of Jesus, Peter and the other apostles answered, saying:

> . . . We ought to obey God rather than men. The God of our fathers raised up Jesus, whom ye slew and hanged

THE BRIDGE OF FAITH

on a tree. Him hath God exalted with his right hand to
be a Prince and a Savior, for to give repentance to Israel,
and forgiveness of sins. And we are his witnesses of these
things; and so is also the Holy Ghost, whom God hath
given to them that obey him.[66]

At Antioch in Pisidia, Paul preached the gospel in the
synagogue, telling the Jews there about Jesus, saying:

Be it known unto you therefore, men and brethren, that
through this man is preached unto you the forgiveness
of sins: and by him all that believe are justified from all
things, from which ye could not be justified by the law
of Moses.[67]

Likewise, when he stood before King Agrippa and related
his conversion on the road to Damascus, Paul told of "a
light from heaven, above the brightness of the sun," and "a
voice speaking unto me." Jesus identified himself to Paul
and said:

I have appeared unto thee for this purpose, to make thee
a minister and a witness both of these things which thou
hast seen, and of those things in the which I will appear
unto thee; delivering thee from the people, and from
the Gentiles, unto whom now I send thee, to open their
eyes, and to turn them from darkness to light, and from
the power of Satan unto God, that they may receive forgiveness of sins, and inheritance among them which are
sanctified by faith that is in me.[68]

Here we must deal with a caveat. We remember that the
"Lord's Prayer" says "forgive us our debts, as we forgive
our debtors."[69] Jesus went on to tell his disciples:

For if ye forgive men their trespasses, your heavenly Father will also forgive you: but if ye forgive not men their trespasses, neither will your Father forgive your trespasses.[70]

Later, Peter asked Jesus how often he should forgive his brother—"till seven times?" Jesus answered saying "until seventy times seven."[71] He went on to tell a parable about forgiveness, which ended with the King delivering an unforgiving servant "to the tormentors, till he should pay all that was due unto him." With that parable as the premise, Jesus said to Peter:

So likewise shall my heavenly Father do also unto you, if ye from your hearts forgive not every one his brother their trespasses.[72]

In his sermon on the plain, Jesus told the multitude:

Judge not, and ye shall not be judged; condemn not, and ye shall not be condemned; forgive, and ye shall be forgiven.[73]

These injunctions are clear and frightening. In every case they condition our forgiveness on our forgiving others. How can we be so forgiving? Answer: only as we follow Jesus as our example. We are told that, while he suffered agony on the cross, Jesus asked his Father to forgive those who crucified him, saying "Father forgive them; for they know not what they do".[74]

Even his prayer on the cross can be confusing to us because elsewhere it seems plain that forgiveness depends upon repentance, and "fruitful" repentance at that. Speaking of some Galileans murdered on Pilate's order as they were making sacrifices at the Temple, Jesus said:

> . . . except ye *repent*, ye shall all likewise perish.[75]

And again, speaking this time of eighteen people killed when a tower fell on them:

> . . . except ye *repent*, ye shall all likewise perish.[76]

At the beginning of his ministry, we are told:

> From that time Jesus began to preach and say, *"Repent:* for the kingdom of heaven is at hand."[77]

At Athens Paul preached the need for repentance.[78] Later, in his defense before King Agrippa, he told of his ministry to both Jews and Gentiles, declaring "that they should repent and turn to God, performing deeds appropriate to repentance."[79] John the Baptist had long before warned the Pharisees and Sadducees to "bear fruit that befits repentance, and do not presume to say to yourselves, 'We have Abraham as our father.'"[80]

So, likewise, when Jesus was teaching forgiveness, he told his disciples:

> Be on your guard! If your brother sins, rebuke him; and *if he repents, forgive him.* And if he wrongs you seven times in one day and returns to you seven times saying, "I am sorry," you should forgive him.[81]

It would help us to forgive one another if we "put ourselves in his shoes" and tried to find a reason for our brother's action. Maybe he fancied that he was just looking after his own interests. Maybe he was ignorant of some fact or facts.

Maybe we appeared to be some kind of a threat to him. Surely he perceived some reason which was valid in his own sight. We must not hold grudges. Grudges cause acid indigestion. Forgiveness flushes out the system. Grudges don't hurt others; they hurt us—ourselves. Neither should we seek to avenge ourselves.

> Do not repay anyone evil for evil, but take thought for what is noble in the sight of all. . . . Beloved, never avenge yourselves, but leave room for the wrath of God; for it is written, "Vengeance is mine, I will repay, says the Lord."[82]

Remember, as one partakes of the spirit of forgiveness, one gets closer to God.

The secret may be that once I sincerely and without qualification admit that I am a sinner, no longer can I expect others to be perfect. So, as I must beg forgiveness for my own wrongdoing, I can accept theirs as no worse than my own and forgive them too.

The effect on our lives of God's forgiveness is to rid us of guilt and depression. It also allows us to forgive ourselves, which is essential to peace and joy. So we cross the bridge of faith, to receive his forgiveness with its peace and joy in this world and eternal life in the next.

In sum, the foundation of this bridge of faith is not our understanding but God's grace. This bridge of faith is built of belief without understanding, like the simple belief of a child. It is held together with mortar of trust, laid on with a trowel of active obedience. Its architect is God, who ". . . is longsuffering to usward, not willing that any should perish, but that all should come to repentance."[83]

> For God so loved the world, that he gave his only begotten Son, that whosoever believeth in him should not perish, but have everlasting life.[84]

Dietrich Bonhoeffer was a young Lutheran pastor in Germany who stood against Hitler. He was arrested, confined, and ultimately executed by the Nazis. While only 39 years old at his death, he had already been recognized as a theologian and had written several books. Of concern to us here is his term "cheap grace," which he applied in the following way:

> Cheap grace is the deadly enemy of our Church. We are fighting today for costly grace.
>
> Cheap grace means grace sold on the market like cheapjacks' wares. The sacraments, the forgiveness of sin, and the consolations of religion are thrown away at cut prices. Grace is represented as the Church's inexhaustible treasury, from which she showers blessings with generous hands, without asking questions or fixing limits. Grace without price; grace without cost! The essence of grace, we suppose, is that the account has been paid in advance; and, because it has been paid, everything can be had for nothing! . . . [85]
>
> Cheap grace is the preaching of forgiveness without requiring repentance, baptism without church discipline, Communion without confession, absolution without personal confession. Cheap grace is grace without discipleship, grace without the cross, grace without Jesus Christ, living and incarnate.[86]

Bonhoeffer says "costly grace" is that which costs a man his present life, but gives him life eternal; and costly because it cost God the life of his Son. Such is the grace upon which the bridge of faith rests.

CHAPTER SEVEN

THE

INCARNATION

C hristians believe that Jesus is the incarnate God. That belief is the foundation belief of Christianity. Simply stated "incarnation" means embodied in a human form or the personification in material or flesh of non-matter or spirit. Christians believe that Jesus was God in the flesh, God-spirit incarnated as a human being.

Practitioners of the other monotheistic religions have difficulty in believing that Jesus can be God incarnate. To make matters even more difficult, he promised to send the Holy Spirit to live within the hearts of Christian people. So monotheists are told that their one God interacts with mankind in three different persons. This is called the "Trinity," and both Jews and Moslems reject it. Christianity is the only monotheistic religion which accepts the doctrine of the Trinity.

Judaism is a monotheistic religion. The Old Testament clearly and unequivocally states, in the words of Moses:

Unto thee it was shewed; that thou mightest know that the Lord he is God; there is none else beside him.[1]

And, again, Moses told the children of Israel:

> Hear, O Israel: The Lord our God is one Lord.[2]

This is called the *Shema* by the Jews, the first word in Hebrew being used to refer to the verse as a whole. It is recited as part of Jewish prayers, included in phylacteries,[3] and on door posts[4] of observant Jewish homes.[5]

Likewise, Hezekiah prayed:

> . . . thou art the God, even thou alone, of all the kingdoms of the earth; thou hast made heaven and earth.[6]

So did Isaiah quote God as having said:

> Ye are my witnesses, saith the Lord, and my servant whom I have chosen: that ye may know and believe me, and understand that I am he; before me there was no God formed, neither shall there be after me. I, even I, am the Lord; and beside me there is no saviour.[7]

As for Islam, the Quràn explicitly rejects the Trinity, saying:

> Certainly they disbelieve who say: Surely Allah, He is the Messiah, son of Mary;[8] . . . Certainly they disbelieve who say: Surely Allah is the third (person) of the three; and there is no god but the one God,[9] . . . The Messiah, son of Mary, is but an apostle;[10]

Indeed, the basic theme of Islam is:

> And your God is one God! There is no god but He; He is the Beneficent, the Merciful.[11]

Thomas W. Lippman explains the Muslim view of mono-theism, and writes of that view:

> What God is not is progenitor or offspring. The Christian
> concept of the Son of God as one with God and equal to
> God is specifically and repeatedly repudiated in the Ko-
> ran, which describes Jesus as a prophet and no more. The
> uncompromising monotheism of Islam is incompatible
> with the trinitarian deity. To Muslims, acceptance of a
> three-natured God is tantamount to worshiping three
> deities, when there is only one. The association of any
> person or object with the Deity is the one sin that Allah
> will not forgive, according to the Koran.[12]

The New Testament is as explicit as the Old. Jesus an-swered a question posed to him by quoting the same pas-sage from Deuteronomy we have seen above. In the Gospel we read:

> And one of the scribes came and heard them arguing,
> and recognizing that He had answered them well, asked
> Him, "What commandment is the foremost of all?" Jesus
> answered, "The foremost is, 'Hear, O Israel! The Lord
> our God is one Lord; and you shall love the Lord your
> God with all your heart, and with all your soul, and with
> all your mind, and with all your strength.'[13] The second
> is this, 'You shall love your neighbor as yourself.' There
> is no other commandment greater than these."

> And the scribe said to Him, "Right, Teacher, You have
> truly stated that He is One; and there is no one else be-
> sides Him;[14] and to love Him with all the heart and with
> all the understanding and with all the strength, and to
> love one's neighbor as himself, is much more than all
> burnt offerings and sacrifices."

And when Jesus saw that he had answered intelligently, He said to him, "You are not far from the kingdom of God."[15]

Why do we need to consider this issue of the Incarnation? Because we cannot escape it. Jesus claimed to be one with God, and he was well understood by the people who heard him. Indeed, they called it blasphemy and took up stones to kill him for it.

Jesus said unto them, "Verily, verily, I say unto you, before Abraham was, I am." Then they took up stones to cast at him: but Jesus hid himself, and went out of the temple, going through the midst of them, and so passed by.[16]

When the Master later said, "I and the Father are one"[17] the Gospel writer says:

The Jews took up stones again to stone him. Jesus answered them, "I have shown you many good works from the Father; for which of these do you stone me?" The Jews answered him, *"We stone you for no good work but for blasphemy; because you, being a man, make yourself God."* . . . Again they tried to arrest him, but he escaped from their hands.[18]

Blasphemy was the charge at his trial. He was asked, "Art thou the Christ, the Son of the Blessed?" And Jesus said, "I am."[19] So, the chief priest called it blasphemy; and they condemned him to death.[20]

Yet neither can we escape the fact that Jesus was human—not God in a mask. He was no spiritual apparition. He was human. He had human emotions: anger[21] and empathy[22]. He was hungry[23], and thirsty[24], and he sometimes grew weary.[25] He was tempted[26] like we are (yet without sin).[27]

He was seen as human by his own family and friends. The people of his hometown asked each other, "Is this not Joseph's son?"[28] They took offense at him[29], and tried to throw him off a cliff.[30] The Scriptures say that Jesus could not do many works in Nazareth, because of his neighbors' unbelief.[31] Even his brothers didn't believe him.[32] After he had called his disciples we read in the gospel according to Mark:

> And He came home, and the multitude gathered again, to such an extent that they could not even eat a meal. And when His own people heard of this, they went out to take custody of Him; for they were saying, "He has lost His senses."[33]

There can be no doubt whatever that his kinsmen and the people in his hometown considered him to be human.

We cannot escape the issue. They thought him human; he told them he was the Messiah of whom Isaiah had written.[34] Either he was deluded, or he was a liar, or he was the Messiah and incarnate Son of God. Each of us, in his or her own mind and heart, must deal with this question.

Paul, who described himself as "an apostle of Christ Jesus by command of God our Savior and of Christ Jesus our hope,"[35] went on to write:

> For *there is one God*, and there is one mediator between God and men, *the man Christ Jesus*, who gave himself as a ransom for all . . . [36]

This is the same Paul who risked his life time and time again to preach that Jesus had risen from the dead, saying, "in Christ shall all be made alive . . . Christ the first fruits, then at his (second) coming those who belong to Christ.

Then comes the end, when he delivers the kingdom to God the Father . . . "[37] To the same Corinthians he had written:

> . . . yet for us there is one God, the Father, from whom are all things and for whom we exist, and one Lord, Jesus Christ, through whom are all things and through whom we exist.[38]

Neither can we forget that Jesus often prayed to the Father. Especially do we remember that at his Last Supper with the disciples he said to them:

> If ye love me, keep my commandments. And I will pray the Father, and he shall give you another Comforter, that he may abide with you for ever; even the Spirit of truth; whom the world cannot receive, because it seeth him not, neither knoweth him: but ye know him; for he dwelleth with you, and shall be in you.
>
> I will not leave you comfortless; I will come to you. Yet a little while, and the world seeth me no more; but ye see me: because I live, ye shall live also. *At that day ye shall know that I am in my Father, and ye in me, and I in you.*[39]

Let us look at the Incarnation as it applies to this carpenter from Nazareth. How can he say "The Lord our God is one Lord," and then elsewhere himself say, "He that hath seen me hath seen the Father"?[40]

First, God is Spirit and, as Jesus said, we must worship him in spirit and in truth.[41] By this primary belief we are turned to contemplate the world of the spirit. We must think of that which we cannot see or count or measure, but which we know to exist because of the material evidence it gives us.

Mind you, now, this is not superstition. Superstition is a belief held in spite of evidence to the contrary. Our belief in the world of the spirit is grounded in evidence we can apprehend by the senses—the material world—which by faith we believe had its origin in creation by this Spirit we call God. That was our subject in Chapter 1 and need not be repeated here. It is enough to say that the marvels of the physical world are evidence of the Spirit's purpose and power.

The world of the spirit is a world of love and truth and light. It is a world of justice and mercy. It is the world of life's highest aspirations; and so we relate these attributes of spirit to God. This is another way of saying that God is life and light and love. It is to say that God is truth and justice and mercy. When we see justice, we see evidence of God. It is likewise with mercy. When we see the evidence of love, we see the evidence of God. And there is no life without the One who breathed the breath of life into all creation.

God is life and light and love—and at the same time all the spirits of justice, truth and mercy—yet he is one God. That being so, why should we be surprised that the incarnation of those spirits in Jesus is still one God, although now in the flesh for a while?

An example from the material world is often used to help us see that God can be Three in One. Early on in school we are taught that two parts hydrogen and one part oxygen make up one chemical compound: H_2O. We also know that H_2O is still H_2O when we see it in any one of its three forms: water, ice and steam. So we can better grasp the spiritual concept: one God can be still God when either Father, Son, or Holy Spirit.

Alister McGrath helps with this concept of the Trinity. He writes:

> ... To affirm the divinity of Father, Son, and Spirit is not to suggest that there are *three* gods, but simply that the one God can be encountered in these different ways, all of which are equally valid. It means that God makes himself available, here and now, directly and personally. There is no point in history which stands outside the saving purposes of God.
>
> The doctrine of the Trinity does not *explain* how it is that God is able to be present in this remarkable way— it simply *affirms* that God *is* present and available in this manner. Any understanding of God which makes it inconceivable that he should be personally present here and now is simply inadequate to do justice to the richness of the biblical witness to and Christian experience of God. The doctrine of the Trinity, like the doctrine of the Incarnation, is not some arbitrary and outdated dictate handed down by some confused council—it is the inevitable result of wrestling with the richness and complexity of the Christian experience of God.[42]

As McGrath says, God is not a committee. The Christian view is that the Father is the God of Abraham, Isaac and Jacob. Since the Incarnation, we encounter that one God through his son Jesus and through the same Holy Spirit experienced by the crowd at Pentecost.

I am an American. I am a father. I am a lawyer. Each of those three terms is descriptive. Each has its own characteristics. Each is an "identity." Each manifests something the others do not, or at least from which the others differ. With all that, I take only one seat at the table because I am only one person.

We no more comprehend the Incarnation than did those who wrote the Old Testament understand manifestations of the Spirit of God. Yet we are told that the Spirit of God "moved upon the face of the waters" at the creation of the world.[43] Bezaleel was "filled with the spirit of God";[44] as were Balaam[45] and Saul[46] and others.[47] Job said, "The spirit of God hath made me, and the breath of the Almighty hath given me life.[48] Ezekiel wrote of having been brought "in a vision by the Spirit of God into Chaldea, to them of the captivity", where he spoke to them.[49] So in the Old Testament, too, we read of God's interactions with men through "the Spirit of God". It is related as fact, but without any "rational" explanation because these are spiritual phenomena.

We cannot *understand* the Incarnation in the same way that science undertakes to understand the physical world. Fortunately for us, there is no requirement that we understand the things of the spirit. We need only to *believe*. This belief, this acceptance of spiritual "things", this faith in Jesus as the Incarnation of the Spirit of God generates our birth into the world of the spirit. I believe this is what Jesus meant when he told Nicodemus, "Ye must be born again."[50]

This incarnate Son of God offered mankind "living water" through the Spirit of God.[51] Those of us who live in a country where there are many fresh water streams and lakes do not easily identify this metaphor with ourselves. But send your imagination into the arid lands of the Middle East, the deserts where people live in thirst. Or think of those hot and dry days when, despite all physical activity, you did not even perspire. Remember some time when you craved water to pour into your parched throat and over your head. Think of the Nile, the Jordan, the Euphrates and other rivers which water the desert lands of the Middle

East. Then, the importance of this metaphor is multiplied, and one better understands the imagery of both "living water" and the river flowing from the throne of God.[52]

Imagery is a part of the Bible. Jesus told his disciples:

> . . . if you have faith the size of a mustard seed, you will say to this mountain, "Move from here to there," and it will move. Nothing will be impossible for you.[53]

I suspect that Jesus refers to the world's mountains as a metaphor for mountains of sin, mountains of guilt, mountains of obstacles, and mountains of doubt. So we learn that even a little faith can remove these obstacles to our peace and joy.

As we saw in Chapter 6, Paul explained to the Corinthians that one must cross this line from intellect to faith, that those who insist that truth is discoverable only through reason cannot "see" into the world of the spirit. He told them:

> But the natural man receiveth not the things of the Spirit of God: for they are foolishness unto him: neither can he know them, because they are spiritually discerned.[54]

And the test of faith we have also seen. Jesus put it thusly:

> . . . My doctrine is not mine, but His that sent me. If any man will do His will, he shall know of the doctrine, whether it be of God, or whether I speak of myself.[55]

He says, in effect, to try the gospel and experience its truth in your own life. Cross the bridge of faith and "see" for yourself.

Of those who depend only upon their own intellect, George MacDonald wrote:

They delay setting their foot on the stair which alone
can lead them to the house of wisdom, until they shall
have determined the material and mode of its construction. For the sake of knowing, they postpone that which
alone can enable them to know, and substitute for the
true understanding which lies beyond, a false persua-
sion that they already understand. They will not accept,
that is, act upon, their highest privilege, that of obeying
the Son of God. It is on them that do his will that the
day dawns; to them the day-star arises in their hearts.
Obedience is the soul of knowledge.[56]

Or, as Jesus said, "Try it, and you will know".

One of the great studies of the Incarnation was that by
J. B. Phillips, who clarified the choice for us when he wrote
of Jesus' claim to be God:

Yet if for one moment we imagine the claim to be true the
mind almost reels at its significance. It can only mean
that here is Truth, here is the Character of God, the true
Design for life, the authentic Yardstick of values, the reli-
able confirming or correcting of all gropings and inklings
about Beauty, Truth, and Goodness, about this world and
the next. Life can never be wholly dark or wholly futile if
once the key to its meaning is in our hands.[57]

So we believe Jesus to be the Incarnation or human embodiment of the very Spirit of God. In the flesh, Jesus is
"the way, the truth, and the life."[58] Through Jesus, man can
see "the *way*"—those *true* spiritual concepts as they are
meant to be manifested in the *life* of every person. If we
imitate his character, we, too, can have the power and peace
of Jesus because we will have the Spirit of God.

You may ask, "Why the Incarnation?" Let me suggest
three reasons. First, the unique embodiment of God in man

through Jesus was provision out of the grace of God for the salvation of those who will believe.[59] The Incarnation led to the cross, and it was the cross of which he spoke when Jesus said, "for this cause" he came up to Jerusalem.[60] He was the Lamb of God, and at his crucifixion, took upon himself the sins of the world.[61] He redeemed those who will accept him as their Savior.[62] His Incarnation was the provision made for our salvation.[63]

Second, the Incarnation is a revelation of the nature and character of God. It provides for us a living human example of the Spirit of God, so that we can learn the lessons of the spirit, both for this life and in preparation for the coming Kingdom of God. These are lessons such as that truth is not dogma, but a pattern for living. And love is not sentimentality, but a tool for living. The Incarnation is to provide Jesus as "the Way" of life, which is the way of worthwhile living.

Third, the Incarnation gives us hope. Through the resurrection of Jesus we can have hope for life after death and hope that good will ultimately triumph over evil. But is the story of the Resurrection true?[64] If it is, then we are hard put to deny the Incarnation. The scribes and the Pharisees repeatedly asked Jesus for "a sign" that he was the Messiah. He told them that there would be no sign but that of the prophet Jonah.[65] This meant that he would be resurrected after three days.[66] On another occasion he said, "Destroy this temple, and in three days I will raise it up."[67] Again, he spoke of his resurrection.[68] *So we come to the factual foundation of the Christian faith: the Resurrection as the sign of Jesus being God incarnate.* Can we believe it to be a fact that he arose? We will consider the answer to that question in the next chapter.

CHAPTER EIGHT

THE CROSS AND HIS RESURRECTION

T he focus of Christianity is on the crucifixion and resurrection of Jesus Christ. By the crucifixion, he paid the penalty for our sin, and redeemed us. That explains the apparent inconsistency between God's righteous judgment of the sinner and God's grace, which provides forgiveness and salvation to the sinner who deserves condemnation. The resurrection is incontrovertible proof that Jesus is the Son of God. Together, the cross and the resurrection manifest God's seal on the New Covenant.

Two sacraments or ordinances are almost universally celebrated by Christians. By the bread and wine of the Lord's Supper we remember the body and blood of the crucified Christ. Baptism represents his burial and resurrection.

We have dealt with issues concerning *what* God did for us, i.e., salvation through faith by grace. Now we shall consider the method chosen by God. That is *how* he was eternally just and righteous while yet merciful and forgiving.

The story of the crucifixion is best told by the Gospel writers. The following is from the New Revised Standard Version of the Bible:

> Now the chief priests and the elders persuaded the crowds to ask for Barabbas and to have Jesus killed. The governor again said to them, "Which of the two do you want me to release for you?" And they said, "Barabbas". Pilate said to them, "Then what should I do with Jesus who is called the Messiah?" All of them said, "Let him be crucified!" Then he asked, "Why, what evil has he done?" But they shouted all the more, "Let him be crucified!"[1] So Pilate, wishing to satisfy the crowd, released Barabbas for them; and after flogging Jesus, he handed him over to be crucified.[2]

Flogging—otherwise known as "scourging" or whipping—is no longer practiced in Western civilization. Many people don't even know what it is. The Romans used flogging whips with "bits of metal attached to them, producing severe wounds that sometimes proved fatal."[3] Here we read the grim realization of Isaiah's prophecy that *"with his stripes we are healed."*[4]

> Then the soldiers of the governor took Jesus into the governor's headquarters, and they gathered the whole cohort around him. They stripped him and put a scarlet robe on him, and after twisting some thorns into a crown, they put it on his head. They put a reed in his right hand and knelt before him and mocked him, saying, "Hail, King of the Jews!" They spat on him, and took the reed and struck him on the head. After mocking him, they stripped him of the robe and put his own clothes on him. Then they led him away to crucify him.[5]

So, as our surrogate, Jesus endured humiliation and torment. Isaiah's description is vivid: "He is despised and rejected of men; a man of sorrows, and acquainted with grief: and we hid as it were our faces from him; he was despised, and we esteemed him not."[6] The Son of God meekly submitted to treatment our law forbids and to which even the most vicious and hardened criminal may not be subjected. *He suffered for us.*[7]

> So they took Jesus; and carrying the cross by himself, he went out to what is called The Place of the Skull, which in Hebrew is called Golgotha.[8] As they led him away, they seized a man, Simon of Cyrene, who was coming from the country, and they laid the cross on him, and made him carry it behind Jesus.[9]

> When they came to the place that is called The Skull, they crucified Jesus there with the criminals, one on his right and one on his left. Then Jesus said, "Father, forgive them; for they do not know what they are doing." And they cast lots to divide his clothing.[10]

> And the people stood by, watching; but the leaders scoffed at him, saying, "He saved others; let him save himself if he is the Messiah of God, his chosen one!" The soldiers also mocked him, coming up and offering him sour wine, and saying, "If you are the King of the Jews, save yourself!" There was also an inscription over him, "This is the King of the Jews."[11]

> One of the criminals who were hanged there kept deriding him and saying, "Are you not the Messiah? Save yourself and us!" But the other rebuked him, saying, "Do you not fear God, since you are under the same sentence of condemnation? And we indeed have been condemned

justly, for we are getting what we deserve for our deeds, but this man has done nothing wrong." Then he said, "Jesus, remember me when you come into your kingdom." He replied, "Truly, I tell you, today you will be with me in Paradise."[12]

Meanwhile, standing near the cross of Jesus were his mother, and his mother's sister, Mary the wife of Clopas, and Mary Magdalene. When Jesus saw his mother and the disciple whom he loved standing beside her, he said to his mother, "Woman, here is your son." Then he said to the disciple, "Here is your mother." And from that hour, the disciple took her into his own home.[13]

When it was noon, darkness came over the whole land until three in the afternoon. At three o'clock Jesus cried out with a loud voice, "Eloi, Eloi, lema, sabachthani?" which means, "My God, my God, why have you forsaken me?"[14]

Crucifixion is a cruel and inhumane means of execution, about which we know only from history. The victim's hands are nailed to the cross-piece, and his feet nailed to the post.[15] The horror of the hammer and those nails driven into his flesh was exceeded only by what followed. The victim hung there, gradually suffocating as his muscles could no longer support his weight. His joints were stretched to the maximum. Painful efforts to get his breath by raising his body on the nails in his hands and feet grew progressively more difficult. The agony was indescribable. Jesus hung on the cross for hours. No wonder that, in his humanity and submission to the will of his Father, it appeared to Jesus that he had been forsaken.

After this, when Jesus knew that all was now finished, he said (in order to fulfill the scripture), "I am thirsty."

A jar full of sour wine was standing there. So they put a sponge full of the wine on a branch of hyssop and held it to his mouth. When Jesus had received the wine, he said, "It is finished." Then he bowed his head and gave up his spirit.[16] Then Jesus, crying with a loud voice, said, "Father, into your hands I commend my spirit." Having said this, he breathed his last.[17]

Now when the centurion, who stood facing him, saw that in this way he breathed his last, he said, "Truly this man was God's Son!"[18]

Since it was the day of Preparation, the Jews did not want the bodies left on the cross during the sabbath, especially because that sabbath was a day of great solemnity. So they asked Pilate to have the legs of the crucified men broken and the bodies removed. Then the soldiers came and broke the legs of the first and of the other who had been crucified with him. But when they came to Jesus and saw that he was already dead, they did not break his legs. Instead, one of the soldiers pierced his side with a spear, and at once blood and water came out. [19]

We realize that it was not out of any sense of pity or kindness that the Jews wanted to hasten the deaths of Jesus and the criminals hanging on either side of him. It was so that their bodies would be removed before the sabbath. Breaking the victims' legs prevented them from pushing themselves up to get their breath. So it led to quicker suffocation. Otherwise, death by crucifixion could take more than one day.[20]

Joseph of Arimathea, a respected member of the council, who was also himself waiting expectantly for the kingdom of God, went boldly to Pilate and asked for the body of Jesus. Then Pilate wondered if he were already dead; and summoning the centurion, he asked him whether he had been dead for some time. When he learned from the centurion that he was dead, he granted the body to Joseph. Then Joseph bought a linen cloth, and taking down the body, wrapped it in the linen cloth, and laid it in a tomb that had been hewn out of the rock. He then rolled a stone against the door of the tomb.[21]

The next day, that is, after the day of Preparation, the chief priests and the Pharisees gathered before Pilate and said, "Sir, we remember what that imposter said while he was still alive, 'After three days I will rise again.' Therefore command the tomb to be made secure until the third day; otherwise his disciples may go and steal him away, and tell the people, 'He has been raised from the dead,' and the last deception would be worse than the first." Pilate said to them, "You have a guard of soldiers; go, make it as secure as you can." So they went with the guard and made the tomb secure by sealing the stone.[22]

It is difficult for us to grasp the horror of the crucifixion. A wounded, bruised victim was tormented with pain and suffering beyond our comprehension. All this was so that Jesus could take upon himself the sin of the world and redeem fallen mankind. As he said when he came up to Jerusalem, he came "for this reason."[23] He foresaw his agony, but said to Peter, "the cup which my Father hath given me, shall I not drink it?"[24] His surrender to the Father's will was complete, and his prayer was "not my will, but thine, be done."[25]

On several occasions, Jesus told his disciples: "the Son of Man is going to be delivered into the hands of men; and they will kill him, and he will be raised on the third day."[26] As written in Mark, we see:

For he was teaching his disciples and telling them, "The Son of Man is to be delivered into the hands of men, and they will kill him; and *when he has been killed, he will rise three days later*." But they did not understand this statement, and they were afraid to ask him.[27]

This was not about Jonah[28] or about rebuilding the temple.[29] He told his disciples in clear and unmistakable terms that he would be killed but rise from the grave.

It is hard for us to believe that on the night of Jesus' betrayal, his disciples "all left him and fled."[30] Peter three times denied even knowing Jesus. There is no indication that any of the disciples other than John was present at the crucifixion. Neither did any of the disciples try to claim their Master's body. The truth is that after the crucifixion they went into hiding for fear of the religious leaders of Jerusalem.

But then the Gospel writers tell us of the resurrection. They do so in these words:

And when the sabbath was over, Mary Magdalene, and Mary the mother of James, and Salome, bought spices, that they might come and anoint him. And very early on the first day of the week, they came to the tomb when the sun had risen. And they were saying to one another, "Who will roll away the stone for us from the entrance of the tomb?"[31]

We cannot help but notice that it was the women who came to the tomb. It appears that the men were still in hiding.

And behold, a severe earthquake had occurred, for an angel of the Lord descended from heaven and came and rolled away the stone and sat upon it. And his appearance

THE BRIDGE OF FAITH

was like lightning, and his garment as white as snow; and the guards shook for fear of him, and became like dead men.

And the angel answered and said to the women, "Do not be afraid; for I know that you are looking for Jesus who has been crucified. He is not here, for he has risen, just as he said. Come, see the place where he was lying. And go quickly and tell his disciples that he has risen from the dead; and behold, he is going before you into Galilee, there you will see him; behold, I have told you." And they departed quickly from the tomb with fear and great joy and ran to report it to his disciples.[32]

John's Gospel tells us that Mary Magdalene saw Jesus, and did not recognize him until he spoke to her by name. She then reported to the disciples, "I have seen the Lord."[33]

Peter therefore went forth, and the other disciple, and they were going to the tomb. And the two were running together; and the other disciple ran ahead faster than Peter, and came to the tomb first; and stooping and looking in, he saw the linen wrappings lying there; but he did not go in. Simon Peter therefore also came, following him, and entered the tomb; and he beheld the linen wrappings lying there, and the face-cloth, which had been on his head, not lying with the linen wrappings, but rolled up in a place by itself.[34]

Then entered in therefore the other disciple also, who had first come to the tomb, and he saw, and believed. For as yet they did not understand the Scripture, that he must rise again from the dead.[35]

Here we face the essential issue. Is the resurrection of Jesus Christ true in fact? Did it really happen? Every person who hears the story must make his own decision; and upon that decision depends his eternal destiny—nothing less!

The Roman centurion and his soldiers were professionals at crucifixion. The centurion assured Pilate that Jesus was dead.[36] He was laid in the tomb. The Jews sent soldiers to guard the tomb.[37] Yet on the third day he arose, and was seen by many of his followers during the next forty days. In his meeting with another Roman centurion, Peter related his experience with Jesus:

> . . . we are witnesses of all things which he did both in the land of the Jews, and in Jerusalem; whom they slew and hanged on a tree: him God raised up the third day, and shewed him openly; not to all the people, but unto witnesses chosen before of God, even to us, who did eat and drink with him after he rose from the dead.[38]

Those who claimed to be eyewitnesses[39] to his appearances after the resurrection gave their lives rather than recant.[40] According to the Roman historian, Tacitus, the Christians were truly martyrs. He said:

> They were put to death with exquisite cruelty, and to their sufferings Nero added mockery and derision. Some were covered with the skins of wild beasts and left to be devoured by dogs; others were nailed to crosses; numbers were burnt alive; and many, covered over with inflammable matter, were lighted up when the day declined, to serve as torches during the night.[41]

These early Christians were good people, who taught truth and virtue; people who warned of Hell, and held out the hope of Heaven to those who believe. They were not the sort of people who could have conspired to perpetrate

a fraud on their friends and families,—especially knowing
the penalties visited upon believers by the authorities, both
Roman and Jewish.

How can one seriously believe their story of the Resurrection to be a fable? Galilean fishermen of that day could
not have made up such a story. Nor did they have a motive
for lying. There was no profit for them in a falsified "gospel."
All they gained from their testimony was ridicule, poverty,
stripes, earthly dishonor, disgrace and ultimately death—
unless their testimony was true and their Lord had risen.

We need not look to the Bible alone for evidence that
the early Christians believed their Lord to have risen from
the dead. Flavius Josephus, a Judean of noble birth who
became a protégé of the Roman Emperor Vespasian, included in his extensive work what has come to be known
as the "Testimonium Flavianum." Josephus was a contemporary of the Apostle Paul. Indeed, he first traveled to Rome
only three or four years after Paul did so. A biography of
this Jewish historian was first published in France in 1989
and later translated into English.[42] The author says:

> So integral is this writer to the history of Christianity
> that the relative obscurity into which Josephus has lapsed
> in our own century can be viewed as another clear sign
> of the de-Christianization of the West.[43]

In *Antiquities of the Jews*, Josephus included the Testimonium Flavianum in the following language, as translated
by William Whiston:

> Now, there was about this time, Jesus, a wise man, if it
> be lawful to call him a man, for he was a doer of won-
> derful works—a teacher of such men as receive the truth
> with pleasure. He drew over to him both many of the

Jews, and many of the Gentiles. He was [the] Christ; and when Pilate, at the suggestion of the principal men amongst us, had condemned him to the cross, those that loved him at the first did not forsake him, for he appeared to them alive again the third day, as the divine prophets had foretold these and ten thousand other wonderful things concerning him; and the tribe of Christians, so named from him, are not extinct at this day.[44]

With all this evidence, it seems only reasonable to conclude that those who professed to have seen Jesus risen from the dead told the truth. And yet such a conclusion on the basis of reason alone is not enough. Simple intellectual assent to the fact does not reach into the heart. It permits, "Okay. So what?" and dismissal of the matter. It doesn't change one's attitude, outlook, and behavior. We have a paraphrase of the French philosopher Pierre Bayle that "If faith says yes to certain ideas, but does not transform the will, its influence on human behavior is small. . . . What reason tells us is one thing, what God reveals is another kind of knowledge."[45]

Cruden tells us that "the word heart is used in the Scripture as the seat of life or strength; hence it means mind, soul, spirit, or one's entire emotional nature and understanding."[46] So Paul wrote:

> . . . if you confess with your mouth that Jesus is Lord and believe in your heart that God raised him from the dead, you will be saved. For *one believes with the heart and so is justified, and one confesses with the mouth and so is saved.*[47]

Belief with the heart makes such belief the basis of every decision one makes, and conforms his behavior to his belief.

The Catholic Archbishop of New York, John Cardinal O'Connor, recently put it this way:

> I don't see how, without the gift of faith, you would believe he (Jesus) was the Son of God. Faith makes the difference. You can study the Scriptures till your eyes fall out, and without the gift of faith, you're not going to believe Christ was the Son of God. The miracle is faith itself.[48]

This "miracle of faith" is available to us through the grace of God, as is the gospel itself. It is the bridge of faith that leads us to acknowledge that his resurrection identifies Jesus as the Son of God. Through the gospel of Jesus we can "see" the nature and character of God.[49]

But why the crucifixion?

To answer this question, it helps to consider the gospel in the context of its historical setting. Jesus came to earth as a Jew. Jewish history was in the Scriptures to which Jesus and his disciples so often referred. The Jews believed themselves to be children of Abraham and the chosen people of God. In Genesis is the story of Abraham, who was told by God to take his only son up on the mountain to be offered as a human sacrifice. On their way up the mountain, the boy asked his father why they were not taking a lamb to sacrifice. Abraham replied to Isaac, "My son, God will provide himself a lamb for a burnt offering."[50] Then as Abraham was preparing to sacrifice Isaac, the Scripture tells us:

> And Abraham lifted up his eyes, and looked, and behold behind him a ram caught in a thicket by his horns; and Abraham went and took the ram, and offered him up for a burnt offering in the stead of his son.[51]

Unlike the pagans of their time, the Jews sought reconciliation with God by sacrifice of animals instead of humans—lambs instead of children. God had shown them a different way. Every Jew knew that story.

When John the Baptist was preaching as "one crying in the wilderness," he saw Jesus approaching and said, "Behold the Lamb of God, which taketh away the sin of the world."[52] After baptizing Jesus, he thereafter referred to him as "the Lamb of God."[53]

Here we become concerned with theological words such as "atonement" and "redemption." They are understandable to us only as we see them in the context of the need for a means of reconciliation with God by sacrifice of a substitute to pay the price for mankind's sin. The Jews understood this because the law of Moses required their practice of sacrificing animals to "atone" for the sins of the people.[54] And we read further in Leviticus about the "blood" of the sacrifice:

> For the life of the flesh is in the blood: and I have given it to you upon the altar to make an atonement for your souls: for it is the blood that maketh an atonement for the soul.[55]

This sounds strange to an American living at the threshold of a new millennium. But the people to whom the gospel was first preached—both Jews and Gentiles—well understood, because sacrifices were an essential part of the religions of that time. Sacrifice was recognized as the means of atonement for sin.

"Redemption" is the payment of an obligation, which then frees someone or something from the claims of another. For example, paying a mortgage frees the property from claims of the lender. Payment of some price to the owner of a slave would buy his freedom—or "redeem" him. It is in this sense that Jesus is called our Redeemer. The cross was the price he paid to free mankind from the power and penalty of sin.

The crucifixion was God's method of redemption, for all who believe. As Jesus said:

> Even as the Son of Man came not to be ministered unto, but to minister, and to give his life a ransom for many.[56]

And Paul wrote:

> For all have sinned, and come short of the glory of God; being justified freely by his grace through the redemption that is in Christ Jesus.[57]

Then, telling of Jesus, Peter wrote:

> . . . and He Himself bore our sins in His body on the cross, that we might die to sin and live to righteousness; for by His wounds you were healed.[58]

And, to the same Christians scattered throughout Asia Minor,

> . . . knowing that you were not redeemed with perishable things like silver or gold from your futile way of life inherited from your forefathers, but with precious blood, as of a lamb unblemished and spotless, the blood of Christ.[59]

God provided the way. The way of atonement. The way of redemption. The way of life. The cross.

CHAPTER NINE

"THE KINGDOM OF GOD IS LIKE . . ."

A fter Jesus was baptized and underwent Satan's temptations in the wilderness, and after John had been taken into custody, Jesus came into Galilee, preaching the gospel of God, and saying, "The time is fulfilled, and the kingdom of God is at hand; repent and believe in the gospel."[1]

Immediately we see the importance of the Kingdom, because the multitudes were told by Jesus:

> . . . I must preach the kingdom of God to the other cities also, for I was sent for this purpose.[2]

Luke has Jesus "going about from one city and village to another, proclaiming and preaching the kingdom of God."[3] Later, the Master sent the twelve apostles "to proclaim the kingdom of God"[4] and, still later, appointed seventy others to go ahead of him and tell the people "the kingdom of God has come near to you."[5]

The Jews to whom Jesus preached were looking for a kingdom to come. They were then under Roman control, which they deeply resented. Their prophet Isaiah had written about a king to take the throne of David.[6] He would reign with righteousness[7] and justice,[8] and in peace.[9] Of that king, Isaiah said:

> And the spirit of the Lord shall rest upon him, the spirit of wisdom and understanding, the spirit of counsel and might, the spirit of knowledge and of the fear of the Lord;[10]

The future kingdom was not a novel idea first preached by John the Baptist and then Jesus. The Jewish Scriptures included several references to a future and everlasting kingdom. For example, one of David's psalms addressed to "my God, O King" said:

> Thy kingdom is an everlasting kingdom, and thy dominion endureth throughout all generations.[11]

The Jews remembered Daniel's interpretation of Nebuchadnezzar's dream, when he said to the Babylonian captor of his people:

> And in the days of these kings [speaking of three more kings to follow] shall the God of heaven set up a kingdom, which shall never be destroyed . . . and it shall stand for ever.[12]

Moreover, they had been taught about Daniel's own dream and its interpretation:

> I saw in the night visions, and, behold, one like the Son of Man came with the clouds of heaven, and came to the

Ancient of days, and they brought him near before him. And there was given him dominion, and glory, and a kingdom, that all people, nations, and languages, should serve him: his dominion is an everlasting dominion, which shall not pass away, and his kingdom that which shall not be destroyed.[13]

But the saints of the most High shall take the kingdom, and possess the kingdom for ever, even for ever and ever.[14]

Daniel also spoke of a resurrection, saying,

And many of them that sleep in the dust of the earth shall awake, some to everlasting life, and some to shame and everlasting contempt.[15]

Even with all this, the people still looked for an earthly kingdom; and hoped that the prophecy would be fulfilled soon, so that the hated Romans would be overcome. The prophets had not been understood; nor was Jesus. As he was crucified wearing a crown of thorns, his accusation read: "This is Jesus the King of Jews".[16] Yet as late as just before his Ascension, the apostles asked:

Lord, wilt thou at this time restore again the kingdom to Israel?[17]

Jesus spoke of the Kingdom in terms completely apart from what we perceive to be time and space. He preached the kingdom of God, not an earthly kingdom in which the Jews would govern. The New Covenant promised the Kingdom to believers, not to the unbelieving Jews. In talking to a Roman centurion in Capernaum, Jesus marveled at his faith. Then, speaking to this Gentile, Jesus said:

THE BRIDGE OF FAITH

> And I say unto you, that many shall come from the east and west, (meaning Gentiles) and shall sit down with Abraham, and Isaac, and Jacob, in the kingdom of heaven. [18]

Only in a Kingdom not bound by time and space could Gentiles yet unborn sit with patriarchs of ages past. So Jesus was not speaking to the centurion of an earthly kingdom, but a supernatural Kingdom.

Jesus told the Samaritan woman that:

> God is spirit, and those who worship Him must worship in spirit and truth.[19]

As to the spiritual nature of the Kingdom, we first remember that Jesus told Pilate, "My Kingdom is not of this world."[20] Further, we read:

> Now having been questioned by the Pharisees as to when the kingdom of God was coming, He answered them and said, "The kingdom of God is not coming with signs to be observed; nor will they say, 'Look, here it is!' or, 'There it is!' For behold, the kingdom of God is in your midst."[21]

So the kingdom of God is spirit, not material. Even if here, it cannot be seen.

Jesus preached with parables and metaphors. That simply means that he told stories and used examples to make his points. He drew analogies from the physical and material to explain the spiritual. He is even recorded as having mused:

> . . . How shall we picture the kingdom of God, or by what parable shall we present it?[22]

But even with his use of illustrations, many of the people did not understand. Like many today, they would not accept anything they could not see and count, measure or weigh. So, notwithstanding the Master's use of parables, they would not believe the spiritual truths he taught.

He had told a great multitude of people "the parable of the sower," following which we read in the Gospel:

> And as soon as He was alone, His followers, along with the twelve, began asking Him about the parables. And He was saying to them, "To you has been given the mystery of the kingdom of God; but those who are outside get everything in parables, in order that while seeing, they may see and not perceive; and while hearing, they may hear and not understand lest they return and be forgiven."[23]

In his parallel account of this interview, Matthew quotes the Master as then saying to those gathered about him:

> But blessed are your eyes, because they see; and your ears, because they hear. For truly I say to you, that many prophets and righteous men desired to see what you see, and did not see it; and to hear what you hear, and did not hear it.[24]

We share their blessing, in that we have the account of his explanations of the parables to his disciples. We, like them, may perceive and understand because the gospel came through Jesus, the Light of the world. We read about the Master's view on this issue:

> In that hour Jesus rejoiced in spirit, and said, "I thank thee, O Father, Lord of heaven and earth, that thou hast hid these things from the wise and prudent, and hast

revealed them unto babes: even so, Father; for so it seemed good in thy sight."[25]

From the parable of the sower we learn that not all those who hear the word of the Kingdom receive it and bear fruit. We, like them, must believe. Believing is seeing. The Kingdom is just beyond the bridge of faith.

So from his teaching and that of his disciples we should learn several things about the kingdom of God. Some, which we consider in this chapter and the next, are:

- It is not a kingdom of this world, but of the spirit.
- It exists whenever and wherever the King's will is done, in love and truth.
- His people have been given instructions and left to be tested for a time.
- The Lord will come again to reign forever.
- His people will live forever in the presence of their King.
- Nothing is of greater importance to mankind than the kingdom of God.
- Its gates are open only to those who have been born again, in and of the Spirit.

In our day and time the words "kingdom of God" or "kingdom of heaven" run through our minds and mouths with little definition. Nowhere in Western Europe or the United States do we now understand through experience what "kingdom" really means—because freedom and democracy let us "choose" our rulers and government officials. In that day the people understood a kingdom to be a city or country in which the king exercised virtually absolute authority. He held the power of life or death over his subjects. We need to change our thinking when we consider the kingdom of God, and think in terms of the age and context in which Jesus spoke. In those terms, God is King and the only choice each of us has is whether or not to submit to his authority. Each of us does have that choice; and upon that choice depends the issue of whether we enter his Kingdom or not. We have no right to argue or debate the issues with God. There will be no Constitution or Congress there. We choose to accept him; or we cannot live in his Kingdom. It is that simple. Those who enter the kingdom of heaven will not find it to be like the United States of America. It is not a republic. It is not a democracy. But this King will govern with justice and righteousness, with mercy and truth. As the Psalmist has written:

> Righteousness and justice are the foundation of Thy throne; lovingkindness and truth go before thee.[26]

In what we call the Sermon on the Mount, Jesus cautioned people to be not anxious about the needs of the body, such as food and clothing, but to seek first the kingdom of God, "and all these things shall be added unto you."[27] Moreover, when he later told a series of parables about the kingdom of heaven, Jesus said:

> The kingdom of heaven is like a treasure hidden in the field, which a man found and hid; and from joy over it he goes and sells all that he has, and buys that field.
> Again, the kingdom of heaven is like a merchant seeking fine pearls, and upon finding one pearl of great value, he went and sold all that he had, and bought it.[28]

To the seventy who "returned again with joy, saying, Lord, even the devils are subject unto us through thy name," Jesus said:

> . . . rejoice not that the spirits are subject unto you; but
> rather rejoice because your names are written in heaven.[29]

Throughout his ministry, Jesus attached no greater importance to any subject than to the kingdom of God or, as he
also referred to it, the kingdom of heaven. It behooves us
to pay close attention to what he said about this Kingdom.

The Scriptures make it clear that the kingdom of God is
not for everyone. It is for those who choose to cross the
bridge of faith, by which there is access to the Kingdom.
Jesus told the parable of a man who sowed good seed in his
field, but whose enemy sowed weeds ("tares") among the
good seed. He said that the sower would tell his reapers,
"First gather up the tares and bind them in bundles to burn
them up; but gather the wheat into my barn".[30] When the
multitude had gone and Jesus was with only his disciples,
they asked him to explain the parable of the tares. He did,
identifying the sower as himself and the enemy as the devil.
The good seed are "sons of the Kingdom", and the tares are
"sons of the evil one". He continued, saying,

> . . . just as the tares are gathered up and burned with fire,
> so shall it be at the end of the age. The Son of Man will
> send forth His angels, and they will gather out of His king-
> dom all stumbling blocks, and those who commit law-
> lessness, and will cast them into the furnace of fire; in
> that place there shall be weeping and gnashing of teeth.
> Then the righteous will shine forth as the sun in the king-
> dom of their Father. He who has ears, let him hear.[31]

He gave another but similar example saying,

> Again, the kingdom of heaven is like a dragnet cast into
> the sea, and gathering fish of every kind; and when it was

filled, they drew it up on the beach; and they sat down, and gathered the good fish into containers, but the bad they threw away. So it will be at the end of the age; the angels shall come forth, and take out the wicked from among the righteous, and will cast them into the furnace of fire; there shall be weeping and gnashing of teeth.[32]

In like terms Jesus later described the judgment, when "all the nations will be gathered before him, and he will separate them from one another, as the shepherd separates the sheep from the goats".[33] Those on his right are invited to "inherit the Kingdom prepared for you from the foundation of the world"[34] and those on his left are sent "away into eternal punishment."[35] How could he have made it clearer that not all shall enjoy the kingdom of God? His descriptions of the consequences of unbelief are as vivid as can be; and those who scoff or turn away do so at their own profound peril.

The Bible is quite specific, both as to who shall see and enter the Kingdom and as to those who shall not. Examples of the latter, who are identified directly or via parables, follow:

- Those who behave like the scribes and Pharisees,[36] who were the hypocritical religious leaders of the Jews.[37]
- The unrepentant Jews, of whom he spoke as "the children of the kingdom,"[38] including their chief priests and elders.[39]
- Those who say "Lord, I will follow thee," but do not; whatever their excuses.[40]
- Those who refuse to trust and to obey as if they were little children.[41]

- Those who refuse to serve him, which is done by loving and serving others.[42]
- Those who refuse to forgive others who have wronged them.[43]
- The unrighteous, whom Paul lists with remarkable specificity.[44]
- Those not born of the Spirit.[45]

Others are in peril, and sternly warned by the Master. They include the rich,[46] as Jesus said after his meeting with the rich young ruler. The reason is most clearly stated in Mark's Gospel, where Jesus followed his first comment with a second:

> . . . how hard is it for them that trust in riches to enter into the kingdom of God! It is easier for a camel to go through the eye of a needle, than for a rich man to enter into the kingdom of God.[47]

We take that to say in another way what he said before about treasures:

> Do not lay up for yourselves treasures upon earth, where moth and rust destroy, and where thieves break in and steal. But lay up for yourselves treasures in heaven, where neither moth nor rust destroys, and where thieves do not break in or steal; for where your treasure is, there will your heart be also.[48]

Financial and other treasures can come between man and God.[49] What better example of material things in which we are tempted to trust? Again and again we are brought back to the true issue: are we willing to surrender all to God, and cross the bridge of faith under a white flag?

Also warned are those who hear the invitation but put off responding until it is too late.[50] These are the people who are unprepared for the sure but unexpected end of time—whether it ends for all mankind or for themselves alone, it matters not which. Jesus called them foolish. In a parable about a rich man whose harvest was so good he felt compelled to build bigger barns, Jesus described the man's attitude:

> And I will say to my soul, "Soul, thou hast much goods laid up for many years; take thine ease, eat, drink, and be merry." But God said unto him, "Thou fool, this night thy soul shall be required of thee. . ."[51]

Likewise, he told a parable of "foolish virgins" who were unprepared for the bridegroom's coming, so were shut out of the wedding.[52]

So some will not recognize their responsibility to hear and to heed the most important warnings ever given. Neither will they recognize that those warnings come from their Creator through his own Son, Jesus Christ. They cling to the material and turn away from the spiritual. When the gates of the Kingdom are closed, they will be left outside; and, as Jesus so often said, there will be weeping and gnashing of teeth.

CHAPTER TEN

"YE MUST BE BORN AGAIN"

Many things in the Bible sound strange to our ears. One of the strangest is Jesus' telling Nicodemus, "Except a man be born again, he cannot see the kingdom of God."[1] This is how it happened. One of the rulers of the Jews was a Pharisee named Nicodemus. One night he came to see Jesus. He probably came at night so that the other Jewish leaders would not know of his interest in this Nazarene. By this time Jesus had become well known to people in Jerusalem because of the miracles which he had done.[2] The Gospel writer continues:

> . . . this man came to him by night, and said to him, "Rabbi, we know that you have come from God as a teacher; for no one can do these signs that you do unless God is with him." Jesus answered and said to him, "Truly, truly, I say to you, unless one is born again, he cannot see the kingdom of God." Nicodemus said to him, "How can a man be born when he is old? He cannot enter a second time into his mother's womb and be born,

can he?" Jesus answered, "Truly, truly, I say to you, unless one is born of water and the Spirit, he cannot enter into the kingdom of God. That which is born of the flesh is flesh, and that which is born of the Spirit is spirit. Do not marvel that I said to you, 'You must be born again.'"[3]

When Jesus uses metaphors such as "the bread of life," "living water," and "born again," he uses them to illustrate the supernatural or spiritual in material terms because these material terms are familiar to us. So he said to Nicodemus, "If I told you earthly things and you do not believe, how shall you believe if I tell you heavenly things?"[4] Here we find one requirement which is essential to our new birth in the Spirit. It is belief—belief in Jesus as the Christ, the Messiah. For Jesus continues in his talk with Nicodemus to say:

And as Moses lifted up the serpent in the wilderness[5], even so must the Son of Man be lifted up; that whoever believes may in Him have eternal life. For God so loved the world, that He gave His only begotten Son, that whoever believes in Him should not perish, but have eternal life. For God did not send the Son into the world to judge the world, but that the world should be saved through Him. He who believes in Him is not judged; he who does not believe has been judged already, because he has not believed in the name of the only begotten Son of God.[6]

Belief leads us to and across the bridge of faith.

We believe that the bridge of faith takes us where science cannot follow. Science is interested only in the physical world—not in the world of the spirit. The theory of science is really pretty simple. The scientist counts how many times something happens; and, if it happens more than half the time, he writes a paper saying that it will probably happen again—if something else doesn't happen. Then he applies for a grant from the government or some foundation to count it again. That is all called "statistical analysis," and it works; at least to keep the scientific papers going out and the grant money flowing in. But science refuses to accept anything it cannot observe, measure, and count. So science denies the supernatural. Science has self-imposed limitations. It refuses to cross the bridge of faith.

For those who would seek the kingdom of God by way of intellectual comprehension or philosophy, Jesus had another lesson. He said:

> . . . Suffer the little children to come unto me, and forbid them not: for of such is the kingdom of God. Verily I say unto you, whosoever shall not receive the kingdom of God as a little child, he shall not enter therein.[7]

Nowhere in the Gospels does the Christ say to anyone that eternal life in the kingdom of God depends upon intellectual comprehension or understanding. He speaks only of belief and faith. The terms are not negotiable. So he tells us to accept them with the innocence of a child.

This takes us back to his interview with Nicodemus:

> Jesus answered, "Truly, truly, I say to you, unless one is born of water and the Spirit, he cannot enter into the kingdom of God. That which is born of the flesh is flesh, and that which is born of the Spirit is spirit."[8]

The questions are: what is meant by being born of the Spirit? and how can that new birth be accomplished? It appears to me that the Scriptures answer those questions in a way which is very simple, but at the same time susceptible to oversimplification. The simple answer is "belief." The complexity arises from the need to believe *in* someone whom we must identify but cannot comprehend with any of our physical senses. Adding to the risk is our need to define what is meant by "believe," and to do so in the context of one's life. Let us try.

First, the dictionary tells us that the verb "believe" can be either transitive or intransitive. That means it may be used with an object or without. The intransitive verb is defined as "to have faith, especially religious faith." The transitive use is defined as "to accept as true or real" or "to credit with veracity"; and it *makes no sense unless it is related to an object.* Accept what? Credit what?

C. S. Lewis wrote about his conversion from atheism to Christianity in *Surprised by Joy*. In doing so, he said:

> . . . It seemed to me self-evident that one essential property of love, hate, fear, hope or desire was attention to their object.[9]

> . . . But a desire is turned not to itself but to its object. Not only that, but it owes all its character to its object. . . . It is the object which makes the desire harsh or sweet, coarse or choice, "high" or "low". It is the object that makes the desire itself desirable or hateful. . . . "[10]

So *what object* identifies a belief as either superstition or salvation, as either nonsense or the new birth? We look again to Scripture:

> Now after that John was put in prison, Jesus came into Galilee, preaching the gospel of the kingdom of God, and saying, "The time is fulfilled, and the kingdom of God is at hand: repent ye, and believe the gospel."[11]

Jesus said, *"Believe the gospel"*.[12]

The dictionary says the gospel is "the teachings of Jesus and the Apostles."[13] It is also defined as "the story of Jesus, the account of the life and teaching of Jesus Christ."[14] Young's Concordance defines the gospel as "good news, tidings, word."[15] Cruden is more specific. He says:

> The English word gospel comes from the Anglo-Saxon *godspel* which meant good tidings, through *godspel*, or god-story. The word in the original (Greek) in the New Testament is *euaggelion*, from which, through the Latin *evangelium*, comes our word evangel, with its derivatives. In the New Testament it is the Christ-message, not the books which were written to spread that message.[16]

So it is good news; good news about Jesus and his Kingdom. Peter and Paul both referred to the "gospel of God."[17] Paul also called it the "gospel of Christ,"[18] and the "gospel of peace."[19] Mark spoke of Jesus having preached "the gospel of the kingdom of God."[20] Jesus himself said:

> And this gospel of the kingdom shall be preached in all the world for a witness unto all nations; and then shall the end come.[21]

The Master also told his disciples that they must *believe in him*.[22] John put it this way:

> He came unto his own [people] and his own received him not. But as many as received him, to them gave he power to become the sons of God, even to them that believe on his name; which were born, not of blood, nor of the will of the flesh, nor of the will of man, but of God.[23]

John tells us of the people coming again to hear Jesus after he had fed the five thousand. Jesus told them that they had better seek the "true bread out of heaven."[24] He said "I am the bread of life"[25] and concluded that sermon by telling the people:

> For this is the will of My Father, that everyone who beholds the Son and believes in Him, may have eternal life; and I Myself will raise him up on the last day.[26]

Later, Jesus went to Jerusalem for the Feast of Booths and:

> Now on the last day, the great day of the feast, Jesus stood and cried out, saying, "If any man is thirsty, let him come to Me and drink. He who believes in Me, as the Scripture said, 'From his innermost being shall flow rivers of living water.'" But this He spoke of the Spirit, whom those who believed in Him were to receive . . . [27]

To Philip, who asked Jesus to show them the Father, his reply was:

> Believe me that I am in the Father, and the Father in me. . . . [28]

Later, Philip preached Jesus to an Ethiopian eunuch, who asked what he must do to be baptized.

> And Philip said, "If thou believest with all thine heart, thou mayest." And he answered and said, "I believe that Jesus Christ is the Son of God." And he commanded the chariot to stand still: and they went down both into the water, both Philip and the eunuch; and he baptized him.[29]

Likewise, Peter's message was "whosoever believeth in him [Jesus] shall receive remission of sins."[30] So, too, Paul and

Silas said to the Philippian jailer: "Believe on the Lord Jesus Christ, and thou shalt be saved."[31]

Using our definition of "believe" in the transitive mode, we see that to be born again one must accept the gospel of the Kingdom as true, and credit with veracity the teachings of Jesus and his Apostles. *Jesus Christ and his gospel of the kingdom of God are the objects of a belief which saves.*

Every person must believe for himself. Parents cannot believe for a child; nor children for their parents. Only in one's own heart can one accept the gospel of the Kingdom as true and credit with veracity the teachings of Jesus and his Apostles. A brother cannot be born again for his sister; nor she for him.

To know the gospel in one's heart as the truth of God, he must experience it. Those people who speak of Jesus as only a teacher do not take him at his word; nor will they respond to his challenge:

> Jesus therefore answered them, and said, "My teaching is not mine, but His who sent me. If any man is willing to do His will, he shall know of the teaching, whether it is of God, or whether I speak from Myself."[32]

If any man is willing to *do,* he shall *know.* This is to cross the bridge of faith, trusting in its reliability because our Lord says we can. This is his invitation to put him to the test.

The first step onto the bridge of faith is to "repent." That means to turn away from self-centeredness and sin to love, to trust and to obey our Creator. *Repentance is another essential to the new birth.* Remember that Jesus said, "Repent ye, and believe the gospel."[33] Repentance involves what the theologians call "conviction" of sin, followed by "conversion." Conviction is produced by the Holy Spirit and can be thought of as acknowledgment and remorse. In other words, before one can turn away from sin, one must accept the fact that he is a sinner. Conversion is change; and here is meant change of both attitude and behavior.

We need to turn away from sin, and to a savior. That requires belief that there is a Savior and that forgiveness is available. We have already seen that the Savior is Jesus, who took upon himself the sins of the world when he was crucified.

> And he said to them all, "If any man will come after me, let him deny himself, and take up his cross daily, and follow me. For whosoever will save his life shall lose it: and whosoever will lose his life for my sake, the same shall save it."[34]

To "deny himself" means that one is to refocus his mind, heart and actions away from self-centeredness. It requires him to look outside himself, so as to see and serve the needs of others. Jesus spoke of the cross as being his purpose; so we understand that for each of us to "take up his cross daily" means to ascertain God's purpose for his own life and to serve that purpose every day. When he says, "follow me," Jesus invites one to do his will and the will of our Father, remembering the "new commandment" that he gave his disciples, which was to "love one another." To follow him is to put into practice the gospel message. It involves a change of values by turning from those of this world to those which Jesus taught.

This is what the Master meant when he called for a new birth, and he plainly told us:

> And he that taketh not his cross, and followeth after me is not worthy of me. He that findeth his life shall lose it; and he that loseth his life for my sake shall find it.[35]

To be born again is to be born of the Spirit. This is the new life one can "find" if he gives up his self-centered life to take up God's purpose and follow his Lord's teachings. We are vain. We decorate and dress the body as if it were the person. But the person—the true worth, which will not turn back to dust—is the spirit. The flesh is only a vehicle for the soul. And God so loved us that, in spite of our sin, he provided the way of salvation for our souls. This is the new birth of the spirit.

Now, we who believe know full well that others think we are foolish or superstitious. Some think we only imagine that there is a God who loves us and deals directly with us on a personal basis. We react to their judgment differently.

Some of us shyly conceal our faith, sometimes in the name of "privacy," for fear of being misunderstood or mocked. This is not enough. We must confess our faith. To "confess" means to acknowledge and speak out; it requires one to take a stand. The Apostle Paul wrote this to the Romans:

> . . . the word of faith which we are preaching, that if you confess with your mouth Jesus as Lord, and believe in your heart that God raised Him from the dead, you shall be saved; for with the heart man believes, resulting in righteousness, and with the mouth he confesses, resulting in salvation.[36]

Remember, too, that Paul was writing to those who risked their lives by confessing their belief in Jesus. There are some believers elsewhere in the world today who are being persecuted, but not in the United States. Here we risk only ridicule or, rarely, anger from those who scorn our belief. We must not be afraid or ashamed, and hide our faith in the guise of "privacy". Nor may we conceal our belief because we "love the praise of men more than the praise of God".[37]

143

Others flaunt their faith, even at the risk of being thought to be self-righteous hypocrites. But, sometimes we turn potential converts to defensiveness by our own aggressive behavior in the name of evangelism. While the Master castigated the self-righteous scribes, he didn't harangue those he had come to save. He showed us that we should kindly share our faith when we find a willing audience. We have a responsibility to be witnesses to others; and we should draw them to the Lord, not drive them away.

We shouldn't be surprised at the ridicule of unbelievers—or even at the malevolence and meanness of some. Jesus told his followers to expect that, and to glory in it. He told them:

> Blessed are you when men cast insults at you, and persecute you, and say all kinds of evil against you falsely, on account of me. Rejoice, and be glad, for your reward in heaven is great, for so they persecuted the prophets who were before you.[38]

Just don't forget that born-again believers are expected to be humble—as a child.[39]

So how do you know if you are born again? So what happens if you believe? So who do you become if you accept the gospel as true?

The answer is that it changes your life. The change shows by the fruits your new life bears. Jesus used as metaphors the tree and the vine. In Luke we read where Jesus said:

> For each tree is known by its own fruit. For men do not gather figs from thorns, nor do they pick grapes from a briar bush. The good man out of the good treasure of his heart brings forth what is good; and the evil man out

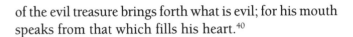

of the evil treasure brings forth what is evil; for his mouth speaks from that which fills his heart.[40]

In his discourse at the Last Supper, he spoke of himself as the metaphorical vine, saying:

> I am the true vine, and My Father is the vinedresser. Every branch in Me that does not bear fruit, He takes away; and every branch that bears fruit, He prunes it, that it may bear more fruit. . . . Abide in Me, and I in you. As the branch cannot bear fruit of itself, unless it abides in the vine, so neither can you, unless you abide in Me. I am the vine, you are the branches; he who abides in Me, and I in him, he bears much fruit; for apart from Me you can do nothing. If anyone does not abide in Me, he is thrown away as a branch, and dries up; and they gather them, and cast them into the fire, and they are burned. . . . By this is My Father glorified, that you bear much fruit, and so prove to be My disciples.[41]

We remember then the parable of the sower who sows "the word of the Kingdom." Only "the man who hears the word and understands it" bears fruit, "some a hundredfold, some sixty, and some thirty."[42]

This is new life in one who repents and believes. The Spirit of truth invades his life. He experiences a change of heart—that inward seat of purpose and motivation. His actions grow more and more consistent with the gospel message and the teachings of Jesus. He learns to love the God who first loved him. His world is turned upside down because things that once were important to him no longer are.

It is about a refocus of interests. Many of those we formerly pursued were innocent but used up too much time, talent, and other resources. It may well call for refocus away from wealth, or power. It may reduce interest in that master time-waster: television entertainment. It will redirect efforts away from social position or other "status" signs. Being born again will shake up one's values and priorities, because he will view his own life from a different perspective.

It's about character. Not just about adultery; but about putting aside lust.[43] Not just about stealing; but about not wanting what belongs to somebody else.[44] Not just about murder; but about not hating others, not disrespecting them.[45]

Even more. It's about love. It's about caring for other people—poor people, ugly people, old people, hungry people, lonely people, even bad people.[46] It's about giving instead of taking, helping instead of hurting. It's about doing for people who can't return the favor.[47]

It's about behavior. Not just about lawful behavior; but about loving behavior.

> Owe nothing to anyone except to love one another; for he who loves his neighbor has fulfilled the law. For this, "you shall not commit adultery, you shall not murder, you shall not steal, you shall not covet," and if there is any other commandment, it is summed up in this saying, "you shall love your neighbor as yourself." Love does no wrong to a neighbor; love therefore is the fulfillment of the law.[48]

It's about patience, kindness, meekness, unselfishness and forgiveness.

It's about a new attitude. It's about an attitude that produces fruits of the Spirit. Paul lists them:

> But the fruit of the Spirit is love, joy, peace, patience, kindness, goodness, faithfulness, gentleness, self-control; against such things there is no law.[49]

146

Elsewhere he wrote:

> For the fruit of the Spirit is in all goodness and right-
> eousness and truth.[50]

And it is about humility, bearing the fruits of the Spirit
to the glory of God instead of to obtain the praise of men.
Jesus spoke to this issue frequently. His examples were giving and prayer and fasting. In his Sermon on the Mount, he
made it plain that the praise of men is the outer limit of
reward for those who seek the praise of men. The rewards
of God are for those who give and pray and fast in secret.[51]
And the higher places will go to those who don't seek promi-
nence,[52] even to those who serve.[53] When we stop to think,
we suspect that ambition is turned on its head for us, like it
was for the sons of Zebedee.[54]

So let us return to Jesus' interview with Nicodemus and
the final words on that occasion:

> For God so loved the world, that he gave his only begot-
> ten Son, that whosoever believeth in him should not
> perish, but have everlasting life. For God sent not his
> Son into the world to condemn the world; but that the
> world through him might be saved. He that believeth on
> him is not condemned: but he that believeth not is con-
> demned already, because he hath not believed in the
> name of the only begotten Son of God.
>
> And this is the condemnation, that light is come into
> the world, and men loved darkness rather than light,
> because their deeds were evil. For every one that doeth
> evil hateth the light, neither cometh to the light, lest his
> deeds should be reproved.
>
> But he that doeth truth cometh to the light, that
> his deeds may be made manifest, that they are wrought
> in God.[55]

Even in our sin and darkness, God extends to us through his Son the love of a Creator/Father. The parable of the prodigal son tells us of the father's joy at the return of one who had turned away from him.[56] The parables of the lost sheep and lost coin tell us of the joy in heaven over every sinner who repents.[57]

And by God's grace we can cross the bridge of faith into forgiveness with peace of mind. We experience a new life in this world with hope. We share joy unspeakable in anticipation of the kingdom of heaven. By God's grace, we cross the bridge of faith out of darkness into light and everlasting life.

CHAPTER ELEVEN

DIVISIONS IN
THE CHURCH

I n today's world we can see religion as an excuse for
hatred between Christians and Muslims in the Balkans,
between Catholics and Protestants in Ireland, between
Jews and Palestinians in Israel, and between Muslims and
Hindus on the Indian subcontinent. We see socio-economic
differences perpetuated and "justified" by religions. Both
the secular world and those who profess some religion ask
the question: "Why do we kill each other in God's name?"

Generally, differences in religions are not only doctrinal, but historical, cultural, and often power-related as well.
The following will touch on some of the reasons for differences, but in this chapter they will be primarily viewed in a
historical context. All will be limited to relations with or
among Christians; and I shall not try to condemn one or
justify another.

In the first century A.D. a major dispute among Christians concerned the issue of whether Christianity was simply a sect of the Jews. Many of the early Christians believed

and taught that circumcision and conformity to the Law of Moses were required of the Gentiles if they would become Christian.[1] Paul writes that his disagreement about this with Peter led him to confront Peter.[2] Not only did Peter hear from Paul about this issue, but we are told that Peter had a vision which led him to the conviction that God offered salvation to the Gentiles upon the same terms as to the Jews.[3] These controversies were settled in a council of Christian leaders at Jerusalem. A letter was sent to the Gentiles with instructions which made it clear that, while the Christian Church was an offspring of Judaism, it was free. On that premise it welcomed Gentiles.

The second and third centuries A.D. saw great growth in Christianity despite periods of terrible persecution by Roman emperors. As it grew, its converts were of necessity drawn mostly from the Gentile world and a background of mysticism, paganism, and philosophy. The converts brought into Christianity their Hellenistic philosophies[4], as well as ritual practices from their mystical religions.[5] Then, according to Gifford:

> Delivered from danger from without, the Church was soon torn by theological dissension within. This had become inevitable, by reason of the changed character of Christianity. Having assimilated Hellenic philosophy and ethics and social forms, she had also come to a new frame of mind, shifting the emphasis from conduct to belief. In no single thing is the change more visible than in the contrast between the Sermon on the Mount, which comes at the beginning, and the Nicene Creed, which comes at the end of this period. The former is an ethical sermon, presenting a new law of conduct; the latter is a metaphysical creed, unrelated to conduct.[6]

In those days as in these, Christians wanted to know what they believed and why. Like us, they wanted to be able to explain their faith to others. They had questions such as: "Was Jesus really God?" "If so, was he really man?" "If so, how could he be both?" Their efforts to understand and explain the mysteries of the Christian faith led different thinkers to different conclusions. So arose different groups who followed different teachers. Examples are: Marcionites, Arians, and Gnostics.

It was in the early fourth century A.D. that the Roman Emperor Constantine was converted to Christianity and issued an edict granting religious liberty to Christians. This put an end to their persecution but it did not solve their internal problems. In an effort to settle the theological questions, the Emperor called a meeting of representatives of all of the churches throughout the empire. They met at Nicaea in 325 A.D. and adopted what has come to be known as the Nicene Creed. Another Council was held in Constantinople in 381 A.D., and the Nicene Creed was modified.

These two Councils did not end the controversies. As explained by an English historian:

> Unfortunately the Church's triumph did not lead to harmony. Even Constantine had found, at the first congress of the Church, that his new religion was rent by controversies. The followers of Bishop Arius argued that, God being indivisible, the Son must be a being later in creation than the Father ("There was a time when He was not"). Bishops of Rome soon claimed primacy over other bishops. Even within Rome, within thirty years of Constantine's death, fighting and bloodshed broke out between the followers of two rival candidates to the Papacy. In the East fanaticism burned in a hundred minor

controversies. All the time, though, the Church increased in size, numbers, riches and influence. . . . [7]

Controversies also arose between the Bishops of Rome and Constantinople. This led to the Great Schism of 1054 A.D.. Clendenin tells it in these words:

> Much like a marital divorce, the schism was a problem that brewed for years. The year 1054 marks only the denouement of a long and tragic estrangement. In that year Pope Leo IX dispatched his legate, Cardinal Humbert, to the Church of the Holy Wisdom in Constantinople. There on June 16, Humbert delivered a papal bull of excommunication that anathematized the Orthodox patriarch Michael Cerularius and with him Eastern Christians. Rome accused the "Greek heretics" of trying to "humiliate and crush the holy catholic and apostolic church," while for his part Cerularius entreated Orthodox believers to "flee the fellowship of those who have accepted the heretical Latins." In the centuries leading up to 1054, political, cultural and theological factors combined to ensure the eventual divorce.
>
> Two controversies, however, were far and away more important than all the others combined. Together they drove the final wedge between Catholic and Orthodox Christians: papal supremacy and the *filioque* doctrine. . . .[8]

There seems to be no doubt but that the bishop of Rome had a "primacy of honor" among the bishops, and was sometimes called "the first among equals."

> . . . The papal claim is the assertion by the bishop of Rome of his authority over the entire universal church, a claim rejected by Orthodox Christians and Protestants. . . .

Friction between East and West usually involved the papal claim.[9]

Further, the *filioque* was inserted in the Creed by the Roman Church without consultation or agreement of the Eastern Church. We need not decide whether the differences were semantic, seriously doctrinal, widespread, or primarily political. The fact is that for nearly one thousand years the Roman and Orthodox churches have gone their separate ways.

The Western church was later split by the Reformation, which was related to the existing political and economic systems, as well as to the Church. In setting the stage to write of Martin Luther, one historian says:

> . . . much of Luther's impact was due to circumstances that he neither created nor controlled, and of whose role in the process of reformation he himself was only dimly aware. . . .
>
> Political circumstances at the outset of the Reformation also prevented Luther's immediate condemnation, and by the time civil and ecclesiastic authorities were ready to intervene it was too late to quiet the storm. On studying Luther's life and work, one thing is clear: the much-needed Reformation took place, not because Luther decided that it would be so, but rather because the time was ripe for it, . . . [10]

The Reformation can best be understood in its historical context. The masses of the people were still ruled by kings and priests, usually allied with each other to maintain power. Kings were to protect the people from enslavement by other kings, and priests stood between them and God. By "divine right" the kings held the power of life or death over their subjects; and, in the name of God, the church could dispense or withhold the sacraments and saving grace. Excommunication was greatly to be feared because "the Church affirms that for believers the sacraments of the New Covenant are *necessary for salvation.*"[11] The Church could forgive their sins.[12] So, to the people, excommunication from the Church meant that they would go to hell.

The Reformation came in an environment of corruption in the Church, tyranny in the various kingdoms aligned with the Church, and a growing belief in the worth and dignity of the individual. Moreover, as Hugh Thomas says: "a case can be made for thinking that the Reformation in the Christian Church, with all its intellectual consequences, could only have occurred after the invention of printing."[13] He goes on to say:

> ... Now the increasing availability of the Bible, the wide circulation of religious polemics and the realization of the differences between the Church's practice and its intellectual foundations transformed Western Christianity. The editions of the Church fathers and the Greek text of the New Testament translated by Erasmus of Rotterdam made evident in 1516 the shortcomings of basic ecclesiastical writings. Erasmus's *Praise of Folly*, published in 1511, satirized all institutions, especially the Church.
>
> The basic Lutheran doctrines of justification by faith alone, *sola fide*, and the priesthood of all believers were an essential corollary of the diffusion of printing. Had it not been for printing, the Church would have been able to crush the Reformation ... [14]

The King James version of the Bible was published in 1611, and Thomas tells us, perhaps surprisingly, that in the third quarter of the seventeenth century nearly forty percent of the adult male population in England could read.[15] The people were reading new ideas about human worth and the dignity of the individual.

Van Doren says that the great concept reborn in the Renaissance was "the ancient idea that man is the focus of human concern". He goes on to write:

> . . . Everyone now had to be able to read the Bible so that he could determine its meanings for himself. The invention of printing made that practical; the translations of the Bible into all the European languages made it easier. Everyone was now his own theologian, and God had descended into the breast of every Christian. . .[16]

Martin Luther, a young professor at the University in Wittenberg, opposed the sale of indulgences by papal commissioners, who took the money of the faithful for a promise that the Pope would see to the pardon of their relatives in purgatory. On October 31, 1517, Luther nailed to the door of his church ninety-five theses. These statements were designed for discussion. "To his dismay they proved to be the opening gun in a religious war, that was to divide the Church forever."[17] Luther's theses spread all over Germany. Finding widespread support, he then began to publish various treatises, drawing his doctrines directly from the Scriptures and denying many of the teachings of the Church. His purpose was not to overthrow the Church, but to institute reforms which would purify it.

Ultimately, however, Luther came to believe that the priesthood itself was built on a false premise. According to Marius:

> . . . Because Luther denied the special priestly status of ministers and made all believers priests, and because he

denied also that the Eucharist was a sacrifice, the altar in Catholic worship was replaced by a communion table set at floor level, and the congregation gathered around the table for the service.[18]

Luther's major premise was that the Christian's faith and practice should be grounded in the Bible, rather than in traditions of the Church. This premise was contrary to the teachings of the Church—then and now. The Catechism of the Roman Catholic Church expresses its teachings as follows:

> . . . the Church, to whom the transmission and interpretation of Revelation is entrusted, does not derive her certainty about all revealed truths from the holy Scriptures alone. Both Scripture and Tradition must be accepted and honored with equal sentiments of devotion and reverence.[19]

The Catechism goes on to teach:

> The task of giving an authentic interpretation of the Word of God, whether in its written form or in the form of Tradition, has been entrusted to the living, teaching office of the Church alone. Its authority in this matter is exercised in the name of Jesus Christ. This means that the task of interpretation has been entrusted to the bishops in communion with the successor of Peter, the Bishop of Rome.[20]

Luther's position "was that the church and the papacy had no divine right in things spiritual; that Scripture, not the priest or the church, has final authority over conscience."[21] "God, conscience, and the Book—on these was Lutheranism founded."[22] From that foundation it is said that "Luther's teachings of *justification by faith* and of *the*

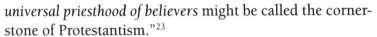

universal priesthood of believers might be called the corner-stone of Protestantism."[23]

As Luther led in Germany, soon Huldreich Zwingli preached in Zurich against indulgences. By 1522 there was a public debate in that city, which led to a government decree that priests were to preach only what could be proved by Scripture.[24]

The practice of searching the Scriptures led to some "theological radicals" who rejected baptism of infants and baptized professing believers by immersion. They were called Anabaptists. The Zurich government held another debate and decided that infant baptism was proper. This brought persecution of the Anabaptists, who "were dispossessed, driven into exile, drowned . . . or burned at the stake."[25]

By 1536 Zwingli was dead and John Calvin was in Geneva, where he soon became the leader of the Reformers. Indeed, the Reformed Church came to regard Calvin, not Zwingli, as its founder.[26] Members of the Reformed Church in France were called Huguenots. In England and Scotland they formed the Presbyterian Church. All were followers of Calvin.[27]

Most of us are familiar with the story of Henry VIII and his several wives. He could not get an annulment of his marriage to Catherine from the pope, even though there were legitimate questions as to the propriety of his marriage to his brother's widow.[28] So Henry had Parliament enact legislation to make Henry himself the head of the Church in England. This led to a separation of the Church *in* England from the Roman Catholic Church and, ultimately, the establishment of the Church *of* England. The last of the Tudor monarchs was Elizabeth I. She was excommunicated in 1570, "for having by force prohibited the practice of the true religion" and otherwise "forbidden the prelates, clergy and people to acknowledge the Roman Church or to obey its orders and its canonical sanctions."[29]

> The popes had often excommunicated emperors, kings and queens, but the excommunication and deposition of Queen Elizabeth of England by the pope, St. Pius V, also absolved her subjects from their allegiance, and was followed by one of the bitterest persecutions the Church has ever endured. To say Mass, to be a priest or to shelter one, was punished by death, and by the most ghastly of deaths, accompanied by torture. Catholics were not freed from some of these penalties until 1829. . . .[30]

While this is no doubt true, the reign of Mary, Catholic daughter of Catherine of Aragon and older half-sister of Elizabeth I, involved persecution of Protestants to such extent that two hundred and eighty persons were burned at the stake and many hundreds driven into exile.[31] She was called "Bloody Mary".

Puritans were members of the Church of England who wanted to purify the Church of all vestiges of Roman Catholicism. Among themselves, the Puritans disagreed about church government. All opposed the hierarchy, but some preferred congregational government while others preferred a presbyterian form. Ultimately, then, the Puritans became either Congregationalists or Presbyterians.[32]

Presbyterians used the Westminister Confession of Faith adopted by an assembly of "Divines" called by the English Parliament in 1643. This was during the turbulent years in Britain when King Charles I and his supporters in the Church of England were in almost constant political fights with Parliament, which had a majority of Puritans. We are told that the King's agents tried to enforce uniformity by use of "the scourge, the pillory, the prison, the cropping of ears, the slitting of noses, and other such gentle persuasives."[33] We also read that "at the same time, with almost unbelievable stupidity, Charles tried to force the Laudian Church on Presbyterian Scotland. The Scots of course rebelled . . ."[34] Ultimately, there was a revolution. Cromwell took over and in 1649 Charles was beheaded. In the meantime, however, the Assembly at Westminster had been named. Most of the Episcopalians refused to attend, and the Presbyterians controlled the Assembly that produced the Westminister Confession of Faith. It was adopted by the Scottish Presbyterian General Assembly, and later by the Parliament in Scotland. The English Parliament adopted it, but the monarchy and Anglicanism were restored in 1660. Presbyterians were again a persecuted minority until the Toleration Act of 1689 granted toleration to all non-Episcopalian "Dissenters."[35]

We turn now to the Baptists, about whom a recent history says:

> The issue of identity constitutes a major problem for the Baptists. Over the past three and one-half centuries Baptists have differed widely about their origins and their composition. Some have the notion that an unbroken line of "Baptistic" churches may be traced back to Jesus and the Apostles (or even John the Baptist!). Others find significant affinities between the Continental Anabaptists of the sixteenth century and the Baptists, so-called, of the 1600s. Still another interpretation is that Baptists arose out of the greater family of English Puritans/Separatists and are traceable to definite ecclesiological roots in that tradition. Finally, there are some modern Baptists who would argue that Baptists originate wherever and whenever the Holy Spirit calls forth a congregation which conforms to

literal Biblical revelation, regardless of historical ante-
cedents or relationships with any other groups. . . .[36]

John Smyth, an Englishman who had been exiled to
Amsterdam, baptized himself and others in early 1609. They
formed the first English Baptist church in exile, having been
Separatists at home. Smyth himself joined the Mennonites,
whereupon he was excommunicated by his fellow exiles.
Led by Thomas Helwys, the exiles returned to England and
became the first Baptist church on English soil. Of them,
Brackney writes:

> . . . Yet, what the congregation lacked in members it
> contained in quality. This first Baptist church on En-
> glish soil was made up entirely of laypersons with the
> officers and pastors also laity. It adopted a general view
> of the Atonement (that Christ died for all) and preached
> heroically in the midst of a great metropolitan area. Al-
> though Helwys and others were imprisoned more often
> than not, neither Puritans nor the civil authorities si-
> lenced the witness. Helwys's great contribution after his
> insistence upon a regenerate baptized church was his
> claim for complete religious liberty. As a libertarian,
> Thomas Helwys proclaimed a beginning of the end of
> the medieval synthesis of a Christian state. . . .[37]

Less than thirty years later, the number of Baptists had
grown and some had fled to the American colonies to avoid
persecution in England.

We tend to think of the "Pilgrims" as the first to bring
Christianity to the New World. Not so. They and the An-
glicans were first in the colonies on the eastern seaboard,
but the Catholics were in America first. Indeed, in 1493
after Christopher Columbus first journeyed to the New
World, the Pope issued an encyclical which divided America
between Spain and Portugal. This he did by drawing a line

from the North Pole to the South Pole running "one hundred leagues west of the Azores and Cape Verde Islands." Then, purportedly in the name of God, Pope Alexander VI gave unsettled lands on the east of that line to Portugal and unsettled lands on the west of that line to Spain. The Pope gave as his reason for the encyclical that missionaries would accompany the explorers and settlers to carry the gospel to the native people. One effect was that the people in Brazil now speak Portuguese while those in the rest of South and Central America speak Spanish.[38]

> Spanish Catholic missionaries began appearing as early as 1520 in what was to become the United States of America, first in Florida, then in the southwestern areas later known as New Mexico, California and Texas . . . . Between the years 1680 and 1793, thirty missions were founded in Texas alone, . . .[39]

French Catholics settled Quebec and the Maritime Provinces of Canada. French explorers were accompanied by Catholic missionaries when they explored the upper Mississippi Valley. In 1634 Roman Catholics founded Maryland, under the leadership of the Lords Baltimore, George Calvert and his son Cecil. The Roman Church grew slowly, until there was a flood of immigrants from Europe in the nineteenth century. By 1995 there were more than sixty million Catholics in the United States, almost one-fourth of all Americans.[40]

The Church of England came to Virginia when Jamestown was settled in 1607. It was sometimes known as the Anglican Church, and later as the Episcopal Church. It incurred great animosity because it was permitted by the colonial government to tax all Virginians, even "dissenters," for its support and to pay its clergy. According to Thomas Jefferson, ". . . the first republican legislature, which met in '76, was crowded with petitions to abolish this spiritual tyranny."[41] More about that later.

The Puritans began the settlement of New England, first as "Pilgrims" in Plymouth Plantation and later as the Massachusetts Bay Colony. They came in the early seventeenth century, out of an environment in which church and state were intimately related to each other. Consequently, they brought that practice to America with them and created a colonial government in which only members of the church could vote and hold office.

> With freedom to pursue an independent course, the early settlers of Massachusetts Bay were in no mood to permit dissent from the "due form" of ecclesiastical government they had established. Having forsaken their homes to found a new Zion in the American wilderness, they saw no reason why their endeavor should be compromised by dissidence. Others, they contended, had full liberty to stay away; and they noted that there was ample room elsewhere in America for them to establish settlements of their own. As early as 1635 the first of a long succession of heresy trials imposing banishment as the most common penalty was held.[42]

According to Paul Johnson, those who returned to Massachusetts after banishment were publicly whipped and imprisoned. Some who repeatedly returned after expulsion were hanged on Boston Common.[43] In time, Massachusetts was made a royal province, and English officials moved in to govern.[44] This brought cultural changes, but not without great stress. Indeed when the first officials came in 1686 and demanded a Boston meetinghouse in which to hold Church of England services, their minister "was straightway refused."[45] Ultimately "the Governor ordered the sexton to ring the bell and open the door" of the Old South Meetinghouse, and Church of England services were held.[46] Royal governance brought with it the English Act of Toleration, which was adopted by Parliament in 1689. Like it or not, the Puritans (who were now known as Congregationalists) had to come to terms with religious diversity in Massachusetts.

The Congregationalists were decimated by the exodus of liberal members to Unitarianism in the early nineteenth century.[47] Most of those remaining ultimately joined some of the Restoration-born Christian churches and some of the evangelical descendants of Reformed and Lutheran churches, all of which came together in 1961 to form the United Church of Christ.

The first Presbyterian Synod in North America was begun in 1716. The Presbyterians had come from England, Scotland, and Northern Ireland. Most of them came to the middle colonies, where there was greater religious toleration.[48] One of their leaders was Francis Makemie who became a hero of the struggle for religious freedom. He was acquitted after defending charges brought by the governor of New York against him for unlicensed preaching. The governor nevertheless required him to pay the costs of the prosecution, so charges were brought against the governor who was recalled to London in disgrace.[49]

Makemie died, and Jonathan Dickinson became a leader in the Philadelphia Synod. For more than twenty years he led the Presbyterians in their debates with the established Church of England.[50] He also negotiated an agreement between the "subscriptionists," who insisted that every applicant for ordination sign the Westminster Confession, and the "nonsubscriptionists."[51] This agreement laid the groundwork for the Adopting Act,[52] which brought the Westminister Confession of Faith to this country.

The Trail of Blood[53] is said to be in its 66th printing, with an aggregate of 2.2 million copies. It purports to trace the history of Baptists back to the days of the Apostles; and it details their persecution, both in Europe and the American colonies. We saw that John Smyth and his followers formed the first English Baptist Church in 1609. Among Smyth's legacies to Baptists and their beliefs was his insistence that "the magistrate is not to meddle with religion." Roger Williams brought that principle to the colonies in 1631.[54] But in Massachusetts the Puritans governed, and Obadiah Holmes was given a public whipping in Massachusetts, because Holmes and two other Baptists had made "an evangelistic visit to Boston."[55] All three were imprisoned and fined. Carroll describes this whipping and Holmes' wounds in great detail.[56]

Baptists have been especially strong in the South among whites and throughout the nation in the black population. They are now the largest Protestant family in the United States, with more than 35 million members. Given their beliefs, this number includes only baptized believers and does not include children.[57]

Like other families, Baptists argue with each other. Their arguments led to the takeover by more conservative Baptists of the Southern Baptist Convention, and ouster from boards and committees of the more liberal members. In its most basic terms, the change was one of power and authority to use the funds allotted by thousands of independent Baptist churches to cooperative programs—such as seminaries, missionaries, and publications.[58] The changes led to formation by "moderates" of the Cooperative Baptist Fellowship.[59]

Another denomination that has come from the Church of England is the Methodists. John and Charles Wesley, together with George Whitefield and others, were students at

Oxford in 1729. These students were concerned with the Church's lack of interest in others outside the Church, so they went out and preached to the masses.

In 1735 John Wesley sailed to Savannah with James Oglethorpe, a founder of the Georgia colony. He began his ministry there early the following year. By August 1737, he was indicted by a Georgia grand jury for, among other things, "not declaring his adherence to the Church of England."[60] After attending court six or seven times to answer the indictment, and in spite of an order of the Magistrates, Wesley "shook off the dust of my feet and left Georgia" to return to England.[61]

John Wesley met a group of pious Moravians on his trip to Georgia in 1736. With their influence, especially after a later meeting on Aldersgate Street in London, John Wesley came to the "warm-hearted emphases on conversion and holiness that still are the central themes of Methodism".[62] Charles wrote the hymns while John preached and, without meaning to separate from the Church of England, they formed Methodist Societies.

> In this entire process, conflicts were not lacking. In the early years, there were frequent acts of violence against Methodists. Some of the clergy and the nobility resented the authority the new movement gave to people from the lower classes. Therefore, meetings were frequently interrupted by paid ruffians, and Wesley's life was occasionally in danger.[63]

By the time of the Revolution there were enough Methodists in the colonies to warrant establishment of the Methodist Episcopal Church in 1784.[64]

Although ill-defined as a "denomination", the Holiness/ Pentecostal/ Charismatic movement has been of great importance in the religious life of America. It started after the

Civil War with Methodist revivals where "entire sanctification" was emphasized. Those who became part of the Holiness movement "believed sanctification was a sudden acquisition by the action of the Holy Spirit".[65] Out of this came the formation of Holiness churches such as the Churches of God and the Church of the Nazarene. Weaver calls Pentecostalism "the lineal descendant of the Holiness movement." It has been said that there are now more than 500 million Pentecostals and Charismatics, a movement which can trace its roots to the "Apostolic Faith Mission" pastored by William J. Seymour on Azuza Street in Los Angeles, beginning in 1906.[66] Pentecostals believe in a gradual rather than instantaneous process of sanctification initiated by baptism in the Holy Spirit, which is manifested by the gift of glossolalia or "speaking in tongues."[67] Prather explains glossolalia and tells about "the massive charismatic renewal among Christians (which) began in the late 1950s and early 1960s when Pentecostalism moved into mainstream Protestant and Roman Catholic denominations for the first time."[68] Growth of the movement is striking, especially if one compares Synan's current estimate with the recent census of almost 9 million members of Pentecostal churches in this country.[69]

Even at the threshold of the twenty-first century we see religious leaders in other countries still making war or negotiating peace with enemies of other religious faiths. In the United States there is no longer the level of animosity—even hatred—once directed toward people who worship in a different tradition. In the next chapter we will consider reasons for this reduction in passions, and suggest a rationale for even better relationships.

CHAPTER TWELVE

"... AND IN ALL THINGS CHARITY"

We have seen some reunions, there have been some mergers, and we hear talk about an ecumenical movement. Even so, the number of independent denominations has increased. In 1997 the Bureau of the Census listed 76 "religious bodies" in the United States; and it included only those "with 60,000 or more (members) as reported to the *Yearbook of American and Canadian Churches*."[1] Some had fewer than 100,000 members, and others reported millions. One had only 28 churches, and three had more than 30,000. Another respected source lists current addresses for the headquarters of 220 denominations in this country.[2]

Christians who go to different churches are likely to agree that our knowledge of God is by his revelation of himself to us. Most would likewise agree that revelation comes via a combination of the elements of the "Wesleyan Quadrilateral," i.e., reason, experience, tradition, and Scripture. But each of these elements requires some interpretation; and the subjective (how it seems to me) is part of the equation in the same way as is the objective (what it says apart from me).

Even those who look to the Bible as authority for all doctrine come away from the Scriptures with different views as to their meaning. Some speak of the "verbal inspiration" of the Scriptures and interpret in a very literal fashion. Some rely heavily on tradition. Beginning in the mid-nineteenth century, others have used "biblical criticism." This is the study of "literary form," along with speculation as to source and "redaction." All of this is considered in the historical context of the environment in which the several books of the Bible are thought to have been written. "Criticism" leads to more liberal methods of interpretation.

The issue is not whether we should *believe* the Bible, but how we should *interpret* the Bible so as to apply its principles, values, and teachings to our lives. This must be done *today* at the threshold of a new millennium. The importance of the Bible cannot be overstated. It can teach us how to relate to God, how we can identify his purposes for our lives, and how we can serve as channels of his blessings to others. But differences in interpretation remain.

Professor Duncan S. Ferguson, in writing of biblical interpretation or "hermeneutics," points out that each scholar begins his work with some "preunderstanding." This he defines as "a body of assumptions and attitudes which a person brings to the perception and interpretation of reality or any aspect of it." He goes on to state the obvious, in these words:

> One's point of view makes a significant difference. Indeed, it would appear that nearly all perception and subsequent understanding and interpretation of reality proceed in some measure from the preunderstanding of the participant.[3]

Then he writes that "since our concern is knowledge of God, the task becomes one of finding the preunderstanding appropriate for such knowledge." Furthermore:

> Biblical witness suggests that such knowledge comes by *faith*. Faith is *the* preunderstanding which is able to rightly grasp God's self-disclosure. Human faith is the correlative preunderstanding of divine revelation. It is by faith that we are able to perceive and interpret the reality of God.[4]

In other words, without faith we cannot get beyond reason.

Another scholar wrote that the interpretation of the Bible "requires a gift of divine grace."[5] He cites the Reformers as believing that it was by the light and guidance of the Spirit that the religious value of scripture could be understood.[6] Moreover, he said that:

> ... the books of the Bible were written in a believing community for believers; they are not "objective" history; indeed their authors would not be flattered to be called "objective". These authors took a stand, and their decision colored every syllable of their writing. ...[7]

Some scholars conceal their "preunderstanding" beneath their academic robes, and present their opinions and speculation as if it were fact. Some are candid. One begins his book by saying:

> ... I should be clear at the outset, though, that as the author of this book, I will neither tell you how to resolve this issue (of how the historical approach affects one's faith commitments) nor urge you to adopt any

particular set of theological convictions. My approach will instead be strictly historical, . . .

. . . I am not going to discuss whether the Bible is or is not the inspired word of God; I will show how we got this collection of books and indicate what they say and reflect on how scholars have interpreted them. . . .[8]

Part of our difficulty comes from the fact that we who read the Bible in English are always looking at a translation. Sometimes the translation is from the Greek in which the New Testament was written. At other times we are looking at a translation of the Greek to English, after an initial translation from Hebrew to Greek, or even from Hebrew to Greek to Latin. The Semitic languages complicated interpretation. Speaking of the judges and the scribes who were necessarily interpreters of the Hebrew text, Kugel tells us:

> Such interpreters were needed even more because of a curious feature in the transmission of ancient Hebrew scripture. The Hebrew writing system was more than a little ambiguous. Like certain other Semitic languages, Hebrew was written down by recording the consonants alone: there were no letters to represent vowels . . . But even within the triconsonantal root structure, context alone will often determine whether a particular word is to be construed as a noun or a verb, or as belonging to one class of verb as opposed to another, or as being in the passive or active voice. Here, certainly, was plenty of room for ambiguity!
>
> What is more, biblical texts were written without the use of capital letters, periods, commas, or any other kind of punctuation. Thus, even where a sentence began or ended was often a matter of opinion: it all depended on how you interpreted it. Indeed, even the separation between individual words was, in ancient

times, frequently left ambiguous by author or scribe. And within the sentence, basic decisions about which words went together with which others and where, therefore, syntactic pauses were to occur—these too were a matter of interpretation.

Such ambiguities might at first seem rather minor, even trivial. However, especially when combined with other obscurities resulting from the passage of time, they created a significant barrier between text and reader. . . . The importance of the Hebrew writing system can thus hardly be overstated.[9]

This is not to suggest that current translations of the New Testament are wholly unreliable. There are now extant over 5,000 Greek manuscripts of the New Testament, some as early as the second century A.D. This is far more than the number of copies of works authored by any other ancient writer; and the oldest copies available are some 700 years older than now known copies of the writings of Caesar, Thucydides, Herodotus, Tacitus and others. Geisler says:

From the standpoint of a documentary historian the New Testament has vastly superior evidence to that of any other book from the ancient world. . . .[10]

Even the recent discovery of the Dead Sea Scrolls, which were written between about 250 B.C. and A.D. 68[11], give more reason for believing that the Bible has come down through these centuries intact than to believe otherwise. Scholars agree that these ancient writings do not change their understanding of the New Testament.[12]

There are, however, some differences in New Testament manuscripts when compared to each other. There are spelling errors and copying mistakes. There are omissions in later manuscripts, and there are words added in later copies. Many scholars conclude that some of these additions and deletions are editorial changes. There can be no dispute that differences exist.

Marginal notes in virtually any modern Bible tell us that Mark 16: 9–20 is not in the oldest manuscripts, which end with what we know as the eighth verse. Likewise, they say, the story of "the woman taken in adultery"[13] is not included in the oldest copies of John's Gospel.

So we have differences in our interpretations of the same Bible. One difference between Protestants on the one hand and Roman Catholics and Eastern Orthodox Churches on the other is who shall do the interpreting. Protestants don't shy away from listening to their ministers, their Sunday School teachers, and others whose opinions they respect; but each Protestant should take seriously his right and responsibility to interpret the Bible for himself. On the other hand, the Roman and Eastern church members depend more upon the hierarchy of their churches and upon their traditions, because the Bible alone is thought not to be sufficient to guide their faith and practice.

Our differences should be considered in light of the experience of the Samaritan woman when she met Jesus at Jacob's well and compared her people's worship of Jehovah at Mount Gerizim with the Jews' worship at Jerusalem.[14] Jesus told her:

> . . . Woman, believe Me, an hour is coming when neither in this mountain, nor in Jerusalem, shall you worship the Father. . . . But an hour is coming, and now is, when the true worshipers shall worship the Father in spirit and truth; for such people the Father seeks to be His worshipers. God is spirit, and those who worship Him must worship in spirit and truth.[15]

Bearing this in mind and remembering Jesus' criticism of the legalisms of the scribes and Pharisees, I suspect that God is more concerned with the spirit of worship than its form. I suggest that he is more concerned with meaning than with method, and more concerned with truth than with tradition. The prophet Micah spoke of his people's worship through the sacrifices of burnt offerings, and went on to say:

> Does the Lord take delight in thousands of rams, in ten thousand rivers of oil? Shall I present my first-born (son) for my rebellious acts, the fruit of my body for the sin of my soul? He has told you, O man, what is good; and what does the Lord require of you but to do justice, to love kindness, and to walk humbly with your God?[16]

Differences flourish in the United States in part because of the separation of church and state. This we owe in large measure to Thomas Jefferson and James Madison. Because of his fight for that principle, Jefferson was called an atheist and an enemy of the Christian religion by the Anglican and Congregationalist clergy of his day.

> The reason for the myth created against him is not far to seek. Just as the landed aristocracy of Virginia pursued him with increasing venom because of his land reforms, the clergy hated him for forcing the separation of Church and State. When he made the fight for this reform, it was a crime not to baptize a child into the Episcopal Church; a crime to bring a Quaker into the colony; and, according to the law, a heretic could be burned. If the latter law was not observed, that compelling all to pay tithes regardless of their religious affiliations and opinions was rigidly enforced. This outraged Jefferson's love of liberty. The Presbyterians, Baptists, and Methodists,

who were making inroads on the membership of the Established Church, were prosecuted, and their ministers were declared disturbers of the peace and thrown into jail like common felons. . . .[17]

Another Jefferson biographer said that destruction of the power of the Anglican clergymen was, for Jefferson, "a private crusade occupying enormous reserves of his energy".[18] Brodie writes about the clergy's virulent opposition to Jefferson when he ran for President in 1800. Of Jefferson's letter to Dr. Benjamin Rush, Brodie writes:

In dodging Benjamin Rush's appeal for "a letter on Christianity", Jefferson wrote, tactfully at first, that he had no time, and that it would do no good. What he was finally moved to write, however, was that he would never court the clergy by offers of compromise. The Episcopalian and Congregationalist churches in particular, he noted, still hoped to be named as the established church of the United States. Each church knew that his success in the election "threatens abortion to their hopes." Then he went on, with that elegant and eloquent fierceness that bursts forth so rarely in his letters, to write one of the most famous of all his lines: "And they believe rightly: for I have sworn upon the altar of God, eternal hostility against every form of tyranny over the mind of man".[19]

In Beloff's book on Thomas Jefferson, he writes of this issue and its consideration by the Virginia legislature. He says:

On June 13, 1779, Jefferson's Bill for the Establishment of Religious Freedom was introduced. This Bill declared religious freedom to be a natural right of mankind, forbade any discrimination between people in their civil capacities on account of their religious beliefs, and left the support of religious institutions entirely to the voluntary action of their adherents. . . . and in 1786 Jefferson's Bill, in a slightly amended form, at last became law.[20]

Ultimately, this led to what we refer to as the "Establishment Clause" of the First Amendment to the Constitution of the United States, through which the people say that "Congress shall make no law respecting an establishment of religion, or prohibiting the free exercise thereof . . .". Madison led the fight in Congress, and that amendment became effective in 1791.

Following the Revolutionary War came the exploration and migration westward of ambitious Americans who owned no land but could acquire it by crossing the mountains into Kentucky, Ohio, and Tennessee. These pioneers were as independent as the original settlers in the seaboard colonies and likewise strong-willed in their religious faith. Preachers came with them; mostly Baptists, Methodists, and Presbyterians. One was Barton W. Stone, who came in 1796 from North Carolina as the stated supply preacher for Presbyterian churches at Cane Run and Concord in east central Kentucky.

Then the Second Great Awakening came to the western frontier. Revivals were held at several places including Cane Ridge. "The Cane Ridge revival, August 7–12, 1801, became the most famous of all. Estimates of the crowd ran from 10,000 to 30,000. Five men were sometimes preaching at once on the grounds. Stone recorded in his autobiography that 'Methodist and Baptist preachers aided in the work . . . and the salvation of sinners seemed to be the great object of all.'"[21] Following that revival, Stone's previous reservations with respect to the strict predestinarianism of the Westminster

Confession of Faith became more intense. That revival had effects even greater than the reported 3,000 converts made.

> One of the remarkable and unexpected results of the revival was the discovery of the fact that in spite of wide differences of belief and polity the members of these three denominations found a common ground of unity in a profound shared experience and the simple, nontheological preaching of faith and repentance. It was, in a way, a practical demonstration of Christian union.[22]

All of this led to the "Restoration Movement" and publication on June 28, 1804 of "The Last Will and Testament of the Springfield Presbytery"[23] sitting at Cane Ridge. It was signed by Stone and five others and it said, *inter alia,*

> We will, that this body die, be dissolved, and sink into union with the Body of Christ at large; for there is but one Body, and one Spirit, even as we are called in one hope of our calling.
> We will, that preachers and people, cultivate a spirit of mutual forbearance; pray more and dispute less; and while they behold the signs of the times, look up, and confidently expect that redemption draweth nigh.

They decided to call themselves Christians and to call their congregations churches of Christ.[24] In 1816 Stone established the Hill Street Church in Lexington, Kentucky.[25]

In the meantime, Thomas Campbell and his son Alexander Campbell likewise "sought to roll back the corruptions of the centuries and restore the purity of primitive Christianity."[26] The Campbells, too, were Seceder Presbyterians who became Baptists. Then they started a movement in Pennsylvania and what is now West Virginia, known as the Disciples of Christ. In 1832 leaders of those two movements met at the Hill Street Church in Lexington and united to form the Christian Church (Disciples of Christ).[27] The theses upon which these Christians agreed was set out in a book written by Walter Scott in 1836.

> . . . The book was titled *The Gospel Restored*, and was the first record by any restorer claiming that there are certain facts, commands, and promises of the gospel. He said the facts are that Jesus died, was buried, and raised from the grave. There are certain commands of the gospel Scott pointed out which are binding upon all that we must believe, repent, and be baptized. And, furthermore, he identified certain promises given in the gospel which are the remission of sins, the gift of the Holy Spirit, and eternal life. All of those elements constitute the gospel, and Scott urged the restoration of that gospel.[28]

This was the first denomination to have its birth in America; and its founders sought union of Christians through "restoration" to practices of the early apostolic church. Unfortunately, near the beginning of the twentieth century, this union began to divide. First, the Churches of Christ broke away from the others, principally because the Disciples began to use instrumental music in worship and had also affiliated with the American Christian Missionary Society.[29] Then in the mid-20s, following a 1917 controversy in the College of the Bible (now known as Lexington Theological Seminary), many Christian churches separated from the Disciples over what they felt was the Disciples' liberalism.[30] These independent Christian churches are more conservative than the Disciples.

We share regret and sadness at the differences among Christians. Especially do we have concern because of the words of Jesus in his prayer at the Last Supper, where he prayed:

> Neither pray I for these alone, but for them also which
> shall believe on me through their word; *that they all may
> be one;* as thou, Father, art in me, and I in thee, that they
> also may be one in us; that the world may believe that
> thou hast sent me. And the glory which thou gavest me
> I have given them; that they may be one, even as we are
> one; I in them, and thou in me, that they may be made
> perfect in one; and that the world may know that thou
> hast sent me, and hast loved them, as thou hast loved
> me.[31]

This concern has led to various efforts at ecumenism. It
has been successful in the uniting of some previously separated churches.

The churches of the first century would hardly recognize the twentieth-century pomp of the Vatican or the icons,
smells, and bells of the Eastern Orthodox churches today.
Yet it is precisely the comfort of familiar liturgy that has
drawn millions to those churches. Nor, on the other end of
the spectrum, would the Apostles see the need to handle
snakes, wear black or collapse in ecstasy as indicia of truth.
Yet those believers who do so are probably as faithful and
sincere as those in the seven churches of the Apocalypse.

There is something to be said in favor of our differences.
A Methodist minister puts it this way:

> By its very nature Christianity is divisive. It forces people
> to choose sides on issues.[32]

And for those who take their Christianity seriously, and
consider its doctrines thoughtfully, he is no doubt correct.
One either believes that in the Eucharist the bread and wine
actually become the body and blood of the Savior, or he
takes the Lord's Supper as symbolic. One either believes in
the need for infant baptism, or he doesn't.

Colaw may be writing to and for Methodists, but his point should prick the consciences of others when he writes:

> ... We have a rich diversity and pluralism in heritage, doctrine, and present practice that constitutes not a threat but a promise. Our controversy, our debating, our varied styles and emphases, our probing and seeking, reflect a healthy body. We are not necessarily one in doctrine, but we are one in hope—that the kingdoms of this world shall become the kingdom of our Christ. And through it all there is, as Paul phrased it, "... the operation of the same Spirit."[33]

Just as the personalities of people differ, so likewise do the personalities of churches,—even within the same denomination. The use of a "high church" liturgy is more meaningful to some people than to others. The "southern gospel" music, which is so precious to some congregations, is thought by others to center upon the worshiper instead of "upon Him who is worshiped."[34] Some churches have no instrumental music, and their congregations enthusiastically sing a cappella in four-part harmony. Others use large choirs and orchestras to supplement the beautiful music of their pipe organs. Many denominations now ordain women to the ministry. Others point to the Apostle Paul's epistle, which tells women to keep silent in church, "and if they desire to learn anything, let them ask their own husbands at home."[35] The emphasis on personal evangelism is such in some churches that "the invitation" is given at the conclusion of every service, while other churches believe it best to invite visitors to periodic "inquirers' classes." Churches differ on both methods and extent of social outreach. While generalities can be superficial and sometimes unfair, it seems plain that churches draw their members from different social and economic classes. Likewise, differences in the nature and extent of education seem to predispose some to their choices among denominations and churches. Neither can it be denied that the minister's personality is the pivotal factor in the choice of a church for many people.

True and sincere worship can be manifested in different ways, and Christians must not forget their Master's command that they "love one another".

There is much to be said for unity; but not for unity in the wrong purpose or for the wrong reasons. We can well understand those who will compromise on some goals and on many methods, but who stand fast when asked to compromise their principles. Indeed, they become our heroes. The challenge is to define the principles so as to not overstate them out of the wrong motivation.

> God is so great,
> His ways are more than excellent.
> God's plan and purpose is so grand,
> He is paramount, foremost, supreme.
> God is beyond our dreams,
> Out of the reach of our imagination.
> His is boundless grace—
> limitless love—
> unspeakable mercy.

No person, no people, no church, no denomination can see or speak the whole of God. Some can see a part, maybe even a part which others cannot see. To use the material only for illustration of the spiritual, those of us on different sides of the planet Earth see plants and flowers and animals not seen in other parts. We see Earth differently. But none can comprehend the whole; nor can any comprehend the whole of God. Each of us must be content with such truth as God reveals to him, through the Spirit of Truth.[36]

To take up sticks and stones—or guns and bombs—against each other in the name of God is to take his name in vain—that is, to take his name *falsely*. Make no mistake about this: one who cloaks evil in the name of God, by hiding political and economic aims behind the name of religion, thereby takes the name of God in vain. The Lord will not leave unpunished any who take his name in vain.[37]

Truth is spiritual and objective, neither material nor relative. So Christian truth is not to be found or decided simply by majority vote. With that caveat, it can be said with some assurance that most Christians and their churches—of whatever denomination—believe what Walter Scott called "the facts, commands and promises of the gospel."[38]

Differences are not necessarily destructive. Yet we need to remember always that:

- There are some essentials to the Christian faith, as to which there can be no disagreement;
- There are important but non-essential doctrines, as to which Christians may disagree and still consider each other to be children of God, beholden to the same Jesus Christ as their Lord;
- There are differences in style—not substance—that appeal to some and with which others are less comfortable; and
- We are commanded to love one another—not just those with whom we always agree.

The concept of disagreement is more palatable, perhaps, to Protestants. Luther taught the "universal priesthood of believers," and few churches came out of the

Reformation with a hierarchical polity. Any who claims for himself the priesthood of all believers is hard put to deny that right to others.

In his wisdom, God may have decided that at this time and place in the history of humankind, it would be better not to have one great unified church on earth. His reasons are beyond our knowing; but we can suggest one. Whether governed by people, priests, or presbytery, a church universal on earth would hold power such as yet unseen in any earthly kingdom or nation. Its penchant for organization of authority would be heretofore unmatched. With such organized power, its temptation to corruption and that alone would be enough to warrant the guess that ecumenism is not in God's plan for this age.

The Moravian Church has only 610,000 members worldwide,[39] but it goes back to the early fifteenth century—a hundred years before Luther.[40] It is "broadly evangelical, insisting on the principle '*in essentials unity, in nonessentials liberty, and in all things charity.*'"[41] That leaves for dispute only the definition and scope of "essentials"; and, even there, it enjoins an attitude of lovingkindness toward those with whom we disagree.

CHAPTER THIRTEEN

THE KING
IS COMING!

There is a Southern gospel song called, "The King is Coming!"[1] To the eye of a Christian living in this wicked world, that song brings a tear of joy.

There will be a day when the Savior comes back to establish his Kingdom. We must be ready! In the meantime, there is work for us to do.

Let me begin by assuring you that I, too, know that questions concerning the Second Coming have troubled thoughtful Christians for centuries. Like some who will read this, I am aware that theologians have critiqued and critics have discounted apocalyptic writings with scholarly explanations and academic speculation. I shall not try to answer all their questions. Nor could I. Some relate to profound mysteries; and we shall have to wait until the End of Time for their answers.

Instead, in this and the next chapter I shall admit to controversies, both in and out of the church. I shall tell you of some of the current dispute concerning the relationship of the year 2000 to the Second Coming. Then I will point to the words of the Bible itself, sometimes in different but well-recognized and accepted translations, and trust that the Spirit will give us such light as is appropriate. That which we leave to mystery, we can leave without regret. We don't need to understand everything. The test of our relationship with God is not understanding, but faith. Our task is to identify and traverse the bridge of faith.

In both the Old and New Testaments some prophecies are explicit. Daniel had a vision in the night, and described it as follows:

> I kept looking in the night visions, and behold, with the clouds of heaven One like a Son of Man was coming, and He came up to the Ancient of Days and was presented before Him. And to Him was given dominion, glory and a kingdom, that all the peoples, nations, and men of every language might serve Him. His dominion is an everlasting dominion which will not pass away; and His kingdom is one which will not be destroyed.[2]

When Jesus was arrested and taken before the Sanhedrin for trial, his reply to a question by the high priest echoed this prophecy of Daniel.

> Again the high priest asked him, "Are you the Messiah, the Son of the Blessed One?" Jesus said, "I am; and you will see the Son of Man seated at the right hand of the Power, and coming with the clouds of heaven."[3]

Those at his trial well understood that answer as his claim to be the Messiah. They didn't believe him and, consequently, found him guilty of blasphemy for having made that claim.[4]

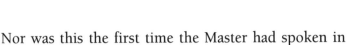

Nor was this the first time the Master had spoken in this manner. He had told his disciples to prepare for coming persecution and tribulation; then said:

> Immediately after the suffering of those days, the sun will be darkened, and the moon will not give its light; the stars will fall from heaven, and the powers of heaven will be shaken. Then the sign of the Son of Man will appear in heaven, and then all the tribes of the earth will mourn, and they will see the Son of Man coming on the clouds of heaven with power and great glory. And he will send out his angels with a loud trumpet call, and they will gather his elect from the four winds, from one end of heaven to the other.[5]

So, there can be no question but Jesus said that he will return in power and glory. Do we not believe him? Can we doubt the Son of God? If this we doubt, what shall we consent to believe? *Dare we not believe?*

The marvelous blessing of his return was promised to his disciples at the Last Supper when he said:

> Let not your heart be troubled; believe in God, believe also in Me. In My Father's house are many dwelling places; if it were not so, I would have told you; for I go to prepare a place for you. And if I go and prepare a place for you, I will come again and receive you to Myself; that where I am, there you may be also.[6]

In the Lord's Prayer, he taught us to pray "thy Kingdom come" and "for thine is the Kingdom, and the power, and the glory, for ever."[7] So, for believers, there can be no reasonable doubt of the future coming of the kingdom of God or of its eternal existence.

Even at the Ascension of Jesus there was the promise of his return. So we read:

> . . . as they were watching, he was lifted up, and a cloud took him out of their sight. While he was going and they were gazing up toward heaven, suddenly two men in white robes stood by them. They said, "Men of Galilee, why do you stand looking up toward heaven? This Jesus, who has been taken up from you into heaven, will come in the same way as you saw him go into heaven."[8]

To the Thessalonians, Paul wrote:

> For the Lord Himself will descend from heaven with a shout, with the voice of the archangel, and with the trumpet of God; and the dead in Christ shall rise first. Then we who are alive and remain shall be caught up together with them in the clouds to meet the Lord in the air, and thus we shall always be with the Lord.[9]

So we find that, over and over again, the Bible through the prophets, the Savior himself, the disciples, and the apostles teach us that Jesus will one day return. Perhaps the most familiar and most puzzling account of his return and the kingdom of God about which he preached is in what we know as the Revelation. While in the King James Version of the Bible it is called "the Revelation *of* St. John the Divine," in the RSV and NRSV it is more properly referred to as "the Revelation *to* John." This is because in both translations the first verse shows it to be the revelation of Jesus Christ by an angel unto John.

The word *apocalypsis,* from which we get the English word apocalypse, means a particular kind of writing or literary form. Those who study the subject seem to agree that apocalypses were written to people being persecuted and in a code which their persecutors would not recognize. The purpose was to encourage the people; to assure them that right would ultimately triumph, so they should wait in patience and in hope. Because apocalypses were written in code, they required interpretation. In this case, the Revelation was written almost two thousand years ago in circumstances far different from those in Western Europe and America. As might be expected, scholars differ as to their interpretation of the Revelation. Not all decode it alike. For example:

> Our interpretation of Revelation depends upon what view we take as to the period of the Church's history to which the figures and scenes preparatory to the climax of the book refer. There have been three chief schools of interpretation. One school (called the "Futurist") regards the book as dealing with the end of the world, and with events and persons which will immediately precede that end. The "Historical" school sees in the book a summary of the Church's history from early days until the end. The "Preterists" look back to the past, and interpret the book as having to do with the times in which it originated. A fourth method sees in the book symbolical representations of good and evil principles, common to every age, and to be understood spiritually. According to this last method, the New Jerusalem, e.g., would be explained as representing the blessedness, even in this earthly state, of true believers whose lives are hid with Christ in God.[10]

Being not qualified to make the judgment call among these various schools of thought, I shall simply emphasize that the Revelation is canonical and accepted by the Christian community. Most of it can more easily be accepted if it is read as figurative instead of literal. Even so, one must not deny its essential teachings or interpret away its truth. Bearing that in mind, let us look at some of its more exciting passages, in which it teaches the resurrection of the dead, the ultimate defeat of Satan, the Judgment, and the glory of the New Jerusalem where the saved shall live forever with God.

Then I saw thrones, and those seated on them were given authority to judge. I also saw the souls of those who had been beheaded for their testimony to Jesus and for the word of God. They had not worshiped the beast or its image and had not received its mark on their foreheads or their hands. They came to life and reigned with Christ a thousand years. (The rest of the dead did not come to life until the thousand years were ended). This is the first resurrection. Blessed and holy are those who share in the first resurrection. Over these the second death has no power, but they will be priests of God and of Christ, and they will reign with him a thousand years.[11]

When the thousand years are ended, Satan will be released from his prison and will come out to deceive the nations at the four corners of the earth, Gog and Magog, in order to gather them for battle; they are as numerous as the sands of the sea. They marched up over the breadth of the earth and surrounded the camp of the saints and the beloved city. And fire came down from heaven and consumed them. And the devil who had deceived them was thrown into the lake of fire and sulfur, where the beast and the false prophet were, and they will be tormented day and night for ever and ever.[12]

Then I saw a great white throne and the one who sat on it; the earth and the heaven fled from his presence, and no place was found for them. And I saw the dead, great and small, standing before the throne, and books were opened. Also another book was opened, the book of life. And the dead were judged according to their works, as recorded in the books. And the sea gave up the dead that were in it, Death and Hades gave up the dead that were in them, and all were judged according to what they had done. Then Death and Hades were thrown into the lake of fire. This is the second death, the lake of fire; and anyone whose name was not found written in the book of life was thrown into the lake of fire.[13]

Then I saw a new heaven and a new earth; for the first heaven and the first earth had passed away, and the sea was no more. And I saw the holy city, the new Jerusalem, coming down out of heaven from God, prepared as a bride adorned for her husband. And I heard a loud voice from the throne saying, *"See, the home of God is among mortals. He will dwell with them as their God; they will be his peoples, and God himself will be with them; he will wipe every tear from their eyes. Death will be no more; mourning and crying and pain will be no more, for the first things have passed away."*[14]

The Apocalypse goes on to describe the New Jerusalem as a city of "pure gold, clear as glass," with foundations of jewels, gates of pearl, and streets of gold. And there will be no night there.

There are those who scoff at this vision, who laugh at "gates of pearl" and "streets of gold." But the size of the city and the materials of its construction are not nearly so important as the promise of eternal life with our Creator, the triumph of good over evil, and the abolition of pain and suffering. The language of the promises is not nearly so significant as are the promises themselves. This glorious picture of the New Jerusalem is our invitation to cross the bridge of faith.

The Kingdom is God's promise through the new covenant, foretold by Jeremiah as follows:

> Behold, the days come, saith the Lord, that I will make a new covenant with the house of Israel, and with the house of Judah: not according to the covenant that I made with their fathers in the day that I took them by the hand to bring them out of the land of Egypt; which my covenant they brake, although I was an husband unto them, saith the Lord: but this shall be the covenant that I will make with the house of Israel; after those days, saith the Lord, *I will put my law in their inward parts, and write it in their hearts; and will be their God, and they shall be my people.* And they shall teach no more every man his neighbor, and every man his brother, saying, know the Lord: for they shall all know me, from the least of them unto the greatest of them, saith the Lord: *for I will forgive their iniquity, and I will remember their sin no more.*[15]

In like manner Ezekiel prophesied, saying in the name of God:

> *Then will I sprinkle clean water upon you, and ye shall be clean:* from all your filthiness, and from all your idols, will I cleanse you. A new heart also will I give you, *and a new spirit will I put within you:* and I will take away the stony heart out of your flesh, and I will give you an heart of flesh. *And I will put my spirit within you*, and cause you to walk in my statutes, and ye shall keep my judgments, and do them. And ye shall dwell in the land that I gave to your fathers; *and ye shall be my people, and I will be your God.*[16]

He spoke of it as "a covenant of peace" and "an everlasting covenant."[17] This new covenant or new testament

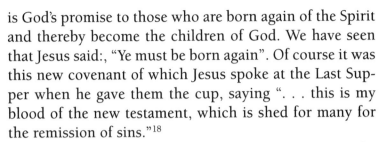

is God's promise to those who are born again of the Spirit and thereby become the children of God. We have seen that Jesus said:, "Ye must be born again". Of course it was this new covenant of which Jesus spoke at the Last Supper when he gave them the cup, saying ". . . this is my blood of the new testament, which is shed for many for the remission of sins."[18]

This is a new birth in the Spirit. Paul explains it to the Gentile Christians in this way, speaking of their relationship with the Jewish Christians:

> But now in Christ Jesus you who formerly were far off have been brought near by the blood of Christ. For He Himself is our peace, who made both groups into one, and broke down the barrier of the dividing wall, by abolishing in His flesh the enmity, which is the Law of commandments contained in ordinances, that in Himself He might make the two into one new man, thus establishing peace, and might reconcile them both in one body to God through the cross, by it having put to death the enmity. And He came and preached peace to you who were far away, and peace to those who were near; for through Him we both have our access in one Spirit to the Father.[19]

To the Corinthians, the Apostle wrote:

> For who among men knows the thoughts of a man except the spirit of the man, which is in him? Even so the thoughts of God no one knows except the Spirit of God. Now we have received, not the spirit of the world, but the Spirit who is from God, that we might know the things freely given to us by God, which things we also speak, not in words taught by human wisdom, but in those taught by the Spirit, combining spiritual thoughts

with spiritual words. But a natural man does not accept the things of the Spirit of God; for they are foolishness to him, and he cannot understand them, because they are spiritually appraised.[20]

In both his Gospel and his epistles, John speaks of those who have been born again as the "children of God". For example, of the Word he wrote:

But as many as received Him, to them He gave the right to become children of God, even to those who believe in His name, who were born not of blood, nor of the will of the flesh, nor of the will of man, but of God.[21]

The Word became flesh that we may have new and "reborn" spirit. As the Holy Spirit came upon Mary so that Jesus would become flesh, so the Holy Spirit begets our spiritual birth, and we are born again in the Spirit as children of God. In this world we are to use the gifts of the Spirit,[22] bear the fruits of the Spirit,[23] and put on the whole armor of God[24] so as "to stand firm against the schemes of the devil."

Because we have been told so much about the "coming" of the Kingdom, we tend to overlook its present existence. But Jesus told the Pharisees that "the kingdom of God is in your midst."[25]

One of the first differences we must recognize, even if we cannot resolve it, is the nature of the Kingdom in this present Age. The Roman Catholic Church explains "the kingdom of God is at hand" as follows:

. . . To carry out the will of the Father Christ inaugurated the kingdom of heaven on earth. Now the Father's will is to raise up men to share in his own divine life. He

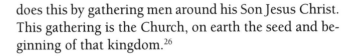

does this by gathering men around his Son Jesus Christ. This gathering is the Church, on earth the seed and beginning of that kingdom.[26]

The Roman Catholic Church teaches:

> Christ the Lord already reigns through the Church, but all the things of this world are not yet subjected to Him. The triumph of Christ's kingdom will not come about without one last assault by the powers of evil.[27]

When the Catechism speaks of the "Church," it means the Roman Catholic Church, self-described as "organized as a society in the present world, . . . which is governed by the successor of Peter and by the bishops in communion with him."[28] Until the twentieth century, it was the papal position that "nobody outside of the Catholic Church can be saved."[29] In fairness, the Catechism now goes on to say of those not Roman Catholic:

> All who have been justified by faith in Baptism are incorporated into Christ; they therefore have a right to be called Christians, and with good reason are accepted as brothers in the Lord by the children of the Catholic Church.[30]

When reciting the Apostles Creed and referring to belief in "the holy catholic church," Protestants mean the "universal church," comprised of all born-again, baptized believers, whatever their denomination.

Dr. Doran recalls the purpose of God, the prophecies of the Kingdom, and Jesus' promises to build his church. He then says that "you cannot escape the conclusion that the purpose was manifested, that the prophecies were fulfilled, and that the promises of Jesus Christ became a reality on the day of Pentecost in the city of Jerusalem in the year A.D. 33."[31]

In its present nature the kingdom of God is not simply a synonym for the church; nor for "the Body of Christ" on earth, as Paul described the church.[32] It is God's spiritual influence which manifests itself in the world, and thereby uses man and circumstances to do the will of the King. In the parable of the sower, we are told that the seed represents the word of the Kingdom. The man who receives the seed into good ground is the man who hears the word and understands it; who then bears fruit, and brings forth, "some an hundredfold, some sixty, some thirty."[33] Jesus also likened the Kingdom to yeast or leaven, "which a woman took, and hid in three pecks of meal, until it was all leavened."[34] We understand from these examples that the kingdom of God now on earth is meant to be an influence which will affect the world. This influence is in the seed sown (which Jesus call "the word of the kingdom"[35]) and the fruits borne by those who hear the word and understand it.[36] It is likewise that leaven is a metaphor for influence.

This is not to say that the church and the Kingdom are wholly separate; but to say that the Kingdom on earth consists of more than the church itself. As explained by a prominent Baptist pastor:

> The "kingdom" is not to be equated with the "church". Actually in the larger sense, the "kingdom of God" is the rule of God in his universe and over all created beings, of which the church is a spiritual element.[37]

Another area of disagreement concerns the millennium, which we call the thousand-year reign of Christ. We read about it in the 20th chapter of Revelation. Some are "premillennialists" and some are "postmillennialists."

Others say that there will be no millennium, and they are called "amillennialists." Premillennialists believe that the Second Coming of Christ will be before the millennium. The postmillennialists believe that Christ will return after the millennium. The amillennialists believe that there is no earthly millennium but that the figures are purely symbolic. I suspect that these disputes will be resolved only at the Second Coming.

> . . . One aspect over which opinions vary widely is the millennium. Many in the Church, true believers, reject the whole concept of a millennium and the rule of Christ on this earth. Other Christians who do believe in a millennium are divided into two groups—those who look for the Church to bring it about, and those who consider a millennial era possible only when Christ returns. Of those holding the latter view, some believe Christ may come at any time, others that the Church must go through some period of tribulation, and still others that the Church at the end of the age must go through all the tribulation, after which the Lord will return. . . . [38]

But even with all the different views as to details, virtually all Christians believe that there will be a Second Coming of Jesus and, at or following that, an end of this world and a new Jerusalem. Given the many times the Bible tells of these things, how can we doubt?

CHAPTER FOURTEEN

WHEN?

In the early 19th century William Miller led a movement of people from several denominations to focus on the Second Advent, which Miller predicted would occur some time between March 21, 1843 and March 21, 1844. When the latter date passed, Miller's associates refigured and re-set the date for October 22, 1844.

> . . . By 1844 there were between 50,000 and 100,000 Adventists in North America. As the day of expectation approached, some disposed of their property, settled all their accounts, and waited prayerfully for the Lord. When October 22 passed with no second coming, vast numbers lost all interest in Adventism and went back to their former churches or abandoned the Christian faith altogether.[1]

Some continued as Adventists. The Seventh-day Adventist Church "arose in the aftermath of what has been termed the Great Disappointment, the failure of the Millerites' prediction that Christ would return on October 22, 1844".[2]

The Millerites were not a cult, as that term is appropriately used; and "Miller's teachings were those of historic Christianity, with the addition of a literal interpretation of the eschatology of Revelation, Daniel, Ezekiel, and Isaiah."[3]

As we approached the year 2000, there was increasing interest in prophecy concerning the end of the world.

Hal Lindsey, best-selling author of *The Late Great Planet Earth*, has more recently written a "revised updated version" of *Planet Earth 2000* A.D.. In it he writes:

> This book doesn't dwell on the past, it looks to the future. Because we are so close to the final, climactic stages of world history, it is considerably easier today for the student of Bible prophecy to see with some accuracy what's coming next. No, I am not a prophet. But I have studied the prophets. And I am certain that all of what they predict for mankind up to and including the Second Advent will occur in the next few years—probably in your lifetime.[4]

He points to signs such as the recapture of Jerusalem by the Jews in the 1967 war,[5] his belief that America is "facing judgment,"[6] a "new world order" originating in the United Nations and the European Commission,[7] famines and plagues even worse than AIDS,[8] persistent violence in the Middle East,[9] and others.

Another writer in this genre is Australian evangelist Ray Yerbury. He prepares detailed diagrams of the end times. In his book purporting to answer "the 77 most-asked questions on Christ's return,"[10] Yerbury writes that the Jewish Temple will be rebuilt on the site of Islam's mosque called "Dome of the Rock."[11] He also says:

> . . . The gold, silver and copper vessels to be used in temple worship are fabricated and available for use. They

are not museum pieces. The writer has had the rare privilege of handling and photographing the complete range of vessels.[12]

Yerbury predicts that Russia will invade Israel, and that "there is another fact that is also certain, and it is that when Russia strikes Israel, God will strike Russia, for Israel is the 'apple of His eye' (Zech. 2: 8)."[13] This he expects "must take place approximately seven years before the return of Jesus Christ."[14] Like others, he writes of the Rapture, the Second Coming, the Antichrist, the Tribulation, the Millennial Kingdom, and the Great White Throne Judgment.

Still another book of this kind is *The End*.[15] Like Yerbury, this American author makes specific and detailed predictions. For example, both write that there will be a seven-year period between the Rapture and the Second Coming.[16] In all fairness, Dobson expresses some reservations. He says, "We have to tread carefully in dealing with the prophecies concerning the end times."[17] He remembers Jesus having said, "No one knows about that day or hour, not even the angels in heaven, nor the Son, but only the Father."[18] And he says:

> We need to remind ourselves that everyone in the last two thousand years who has predicted a specific time for the end of the world has been wrong.[19]

This does not keep him from listing what he refers to as "fifty remarkable events pointing toward the end."[20]

Of course not all writers share the views of Lindsey, Yerbury, and Dobson. On the contrary, there are others who imply a contrary view while examining the recent and current concern about eschatology. So we can read in a collection of academic papers the following:

> . . . "Decentering" trends in culture lead to apocalypticism as the waning of the cultural center stimulates a perception of the imminent end of culture. Millennialist fundamentalist visions look toward an ultimate post-apocalyptic recentering of culture. However, the American apocalyptic excitation cuts across sectarian differences and can be discerned in Protestant, Catholic, Jewish, Islamic, and Mormon contexts. Additionally it transcends the increasingly ambiguous boundary between "sacred" and "secular" realms. . . . [21]

The plan of their book is revealed in the description of its sections, which are: "theoretical issues in the study and basic conceptualization of apocalypticism and millenarianism," "contemporary secularization of millenarianism and the interplay of 'religious' and 'secular' elements in particular movements and activist milieux," "apocalyptic and millenarian ferment across the spectrum of American institutionalized religion," and "issues of violence and confrontation."[22]

One cannot help but be impressed—even amazed—at the erudition of editors who can string together so many multi-syllables. Their explanation and comments are more arcane than is the apocalyptic literature itself. One must also be impressed with the number of academics and social scientists who were recruited to contribute to the book. They included sociologists, political scientists, PhD students, and even an ethnomusicologist. A few teach "religious studies," but none was identified as a theologian.

Contemporary interest in the coming millineum has led to publication of fictional bestsellers concerning the apocalypse. The *Left Behind* series of four books by Tim LaHaye and Jerry B. Jenkins "are intended to appeal not only to committed Christians, but also to half-hearted churchgoers and skeptical seculars."[23] According to a newspaper article, "the books have crossed over to a broader audience, attracting even secular readers with thriller-type prose."[24] These books have sold nearly 3 million copies, and:

> The series made publishing history in September when all four of the books ascended to the top four slots on Publishers Weekly magazine's lists of religion best sellers in hardcover and paperback.[25]

There seems to be no doubt as to the popular interest in this subject, and the interest is not confined solely to "fundamentalist and evangelistic Christians."

Margaret Nutting Ralph writes of "literary forms"; and so she has several differences with others in interpretation of eschatology. However, to her book she adds an Endnote, in which she writes:

> "Are you denying the Second Coming?" is a question which I am often asked. My answer is, "No, I am not." A belief in a future culminating event is core to Christianity. We profess our belief in such an event when we say in the Creed that Jesus "ascended into heaven, and is seated at the right hand of the Father. He will come again in glory to judge the living and the dead."[26]

It is Mrs. Ralph's thesis that:

> There are three contexts which must be considered in order to determine the revelation which any passage of Scripture is teaching. These contexts are the literary form, the beliefs of the time, and the process of revelation.[27]

Her premise is that an "apocalypse" or "revelation" is written to a people who are at the time being persecuted, with a purpose to offer them hope of an end to their persecution and ultimate victory. Because it is to be distributed during the time of their persecution, it is written in a "code" which they well understand but their persecutors do not. She proceeds to decode the apocalyptic writings. Her message is summed up as follows:

> So far we have seen that the core good news of Scripture, both Old Testament and New, is that God is love. We have seen that we do not have to earn this love. It is given to us as a gift. We need only respond with faith and love. Nor do we have any reason to fear judgment. While the inevitable ramification of sin is suffering, it is God's will that we be reconciled and saved. Since we are loved, we are required to love others, even our enemies, not out of fear of punishment but just because love begets love.[28]

Mrs. Ralph concludes her Endnote as follows:

> . . . Jesus is already present among us. . . . The risen Christ is present with us, just as he was present with the disciples on the road to Emmaus. We have nothing to fear, not even the end of the world.[29]

Then there are some who view the apocalypse with derision. Clark Morphew denies mocking the Scriptures but he writes:

> . . . Some believe a great tribulation will occur after Jesus rides in and rounds up all the true believers into that great corral in the sky . . .
> Imagine a vehicle with a carload of passengers zooming along a busy interstate. Two of those people rise with Christ into heaven, two remain in the car. Imagine the

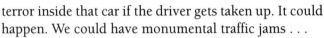

terror inside that car if the driver gets taken up. It could happen. We could have monumental traffic jams . . .

A woman hanging clothes in the back yard sees a big shadow obliterating the sun. She looks to the sky and sees Jesus just hanging like an acrobat on a wire. She looks at Him for a moment, exclaims, then runs into the house to call Marge, the neighbor.[30]

Morphew is "an ordained clergyman."[31] Perhaps in this era we should be surprised only that his column appears in a section of the paper called "Faith & Values."

To the question, "Will Jesus come again in glory with his angels?" the answer to Bible-believers is an unqualified "Yes!" To the question, "When will this be?" the answer is "the Father alone knows."

We know that the early Christians expected the Second Coming in their own generation. No doubt they did so because of what their Lord had said in his discourse on the Mount of Olives. There he had said two things which appear to contradict each other. After telling them of things which will happen before he returns, he said:

Truly I say to you, this generation will not pass away until all these things take place. Heaven and earth will pass away, but My words shall not pass away. But of that day and hour no one knows, not even the angels of heaven, nor the Son, but the Father alone.[32]

To add to our confusion he had said before:

Truly I say to you, there are some of those who are standing here who shall not taste death until they see the Son of Man coming in His kingdom.[33]

Yet he had also said to them:

> And this gospel of the kingdom shall be preached in the whole world for a witness to all the nations, and then the end shall come.[34]

Some would say that "this generation" may mean "this race."[35] Others disagree.[36] Obviously, this is a very difficult question for many. Speaking of Mark 13:30, C. S. Lewis deals with the problem in this fashion:

> It is certainly the most embarrassing verse in the Bible. Yet how teasing, also, that within fourteen words of it should come the statement "But of that day and that hour knoweth no man, no, not the angels which are in heaven, neither the Son, but the Father." The one exhibition of error and the one confession of ignorance grow side by side. That they stood thus in the mouth of Jesus himself, and were not merely placed thus by the reporter, we surely need not doubt. Unless the reporter were perfectly honest he would never have recorded the confession of ignorance at all; he could have had no motive for doing so except a desire to tell the whole truth. And unless later copyists were equally honest, they would never have preserved the (apparently) mistaken prediction about "this generation" after the passage of time had shown the (apparent) mistake. This passage (Mark 13: 30–32) and the cry "Why hast thou forsaken me?" (Mark 15: 34) together make up the strongest proof that the New Testament is historically reliable. The evangelists have the first great characteristic of honest witnesses: They mention facts which are, at first sight, damaging to their main contention.[37]

Paul undertook to explain to the Thessalonians that the day of the Lord had not come.[38] Indeed, he told them that there would be apostasy first, and then a "man of lawlessness" to be slain by the Lord on his return.[39]

What we refer to as the "Olivet Discourse" is recorded in both Matthew and Mark. Both say this took place on the Mount of Olives. Jesus and his disciples had just left the temple where Jesus had told them that the temple would be destroyed. We know that the temple was destroyed by the Romans about 35 years later. Our confusion comes because both of the Gospel writers tell next about the "Olivet Discourse," where the disciples asked Jesus when "these things" would be. Readers disagree as to how much of Jesus' answer to his disciples' questions concerns the destruction of Jerusalem and how much concerns his Second Coming, about which Matthew says the disciples specifically asked. He told them of their coming persecution, false prophets, and the Great Tribulation. He described his Second Advent but then said to them:

> But of that day and hour no one knows, neither the angels of heaven, nor the Son, but the Father alone. For as it was in the days of Noah, so it will be at the coming of the Son of Man. In those days before the flood, they were eating and drinking, marrying and giving in marriage, up to the day that Noah entered the ark. They did not know until the flood came and carried them all away. So will it be also at the coming of the Son of Man.[40]

In the account by Mark, he continues directly with this injunction:

> Be watchful! Be alert! You do not know when the time will come. It is like a man traveling abroad. He leaves home and places his servants in charge, each with his work, and orders the gatekeeper to be on the watch.

> Watch, therefore; you do not know when the lord of the
> house is coming, whether in the evening, or at midnight,
> or at cockcrow, or in the morning. May he not come
> suddenly and find you sleeping. What I say to you, I say
> to all: "Watch!"[41]

We are reminded of the message God gives us through the
prophet Ezekiel where it is written:

> Son of Man, I have made thee a watchman unto the house
> of Israel; therefore hear the word at my mouth, and give
> them warning from me. When I say unto the wicked,
> thou shalt surely die; and thou givest him not warning,
> nor speakest to warn the wicked from his wicked way,
> to save his life; the same wicked man shall die in his
> iniquity; but his blood will I require at thine hand. Yet if
> thou warn the wicked, and he turn not from his wicked-
> ness, nor from his wicked way, he shall die in his iniq-
> uity; but thou hast delivered thy soul.[42]

So we are to watch for the Second Coming and warn others
by both precept and example that, without repentance and
faith, they shall perish.

The equally pressing question for each of us should be,
"Will the world end for me?" The unqualified answer to
that question is, "Yes." There will be a day when the world
will end for me, whether at the Rapture or at my death. I do
not know when that will be, but I cannot doubt that the
end will come for me. Obviously, the same is true for you.
Permit me, if you please, two personal stories to illustrate
the immutable truth of these facts.

In November 1951 my father called me aside privately
to tell me that a doctor had examined him during the previous week and diagnosed lung cancer. The doctor had

told him that he then had less than 60 days to live. Needless to say, on the following day I went with him to see another doctor for a second opinion. The second doctor examined him carefully and then told him, "Joe, you do not have lung cancer. The X-ray evidence is of calcification, which many people in this area have." Then he added, somewhat in jest, "You will not die in the next sixty days, unless you're killed in an automobile accident." We left the doctor's office greatly relieved. On December 16, 1951, my father was killed instantly in an automobile wreck. The point is not the doctor's remark. The point is the uncertainty of life.

Ten years ago, after an operation for colon cancer, I was told by my surgeon that the cancer had metastasized outside the colon so that I could not expect to live another year. My surgeon believed that; and so did I. I dissolved my law partnership, and put my affairs "in order." But he continued to treat me—as did other doctors. They put me on chemotherapy for a year. I didn't die. I came to know that God's purpose for my life had not been fully realized. Maybe God wants me to write.

Most of us have had experiences similar to these. If not, we know people who have had similar experiences. Sometimes, we need to reflect. Every "survivor" with whom I've talked about cancer agrees that it gave him or her a new perception of life and the meaning of life.

Believe, if you will, that the world will end at the day forecast by some self-proclaimed prophet. Or believe that even Jesus didn't know when the world will end. Whichever you believe, know without question that you will not live in this world forever; and that you could die tomorrow—or even today.

Given these uncertainties of interpretation, we turn to the reassurance of Apostolic epistles. For example, Peter wrote:

> Know this first of all, that in the last days mockers will come with their mocking, following after their own lusts, and saying, "Where is the promise of His coming? For ever since the fathers fell asleep, all continues just as it was from the beginning of creation". For when they maintain this, it escapes their notice that by the word of God the heavens existed long ago and the earth was formed out of water and by water, through which the world at that time was destroyed, being flooded with water. But the present heavens and earth by His word are being reserved for fire, kept for the day of judgment and destruction of ungodly men. But do not let this one fact escape your notice, beloved, that with the Lord one day is as a thousand years, and a thousand years as one day. *The Lord is not slow about His promise, as some count slowness, but is patient toward you, not wishing for any to perish but for all to come to repentance.*[43]

> . . . But according to His promise we are looking for new heavens and a new earth, in which righteousness dwells.[44]

So we also read in the epistle of James his encouragement to patience, he having written:

> Be patient, therefore, brethren, until the coming of the Lord. Behold, the farmer waits for the precious produce of the soil, being patient about it, until it gets the early and late rains. You too be patient; strengthen your hearts, for the coming of the Lord is at hand.[45]

We must be satisfied that none of us knows when our Lord will return. It is enough to know that we must be always ready for his coming.

Even secular futurists hold out hope for mankind's future. We read:

> At the dawn of the third millennium there are unmistakable signs of a worldwide multidenominational religious revival.[46]

They conclude their chapter on "Religious Revival of the Third Millennium" with these observations:

> As the symbolic year 2000 approaches, humanity is not abandoning science, but through this religious revival, we are reaffirming the spiritual in what is now a more balanced quest to better our lives and those of our neighbors.[47]

If you have found the bridge of faith and started across it—then you believe the promises of eternal life. So long as you remain in this world, it is your job to give your life's service to the gospel of the Kingdom and be ready for him to come again, "like a thief in the night."

If you have not found the bridge of faith or if you have found some reason or excuse to put off entering upon it, be warned! *Be warned*! Your own eternal destiny is at stake. Don't wait another day!

"LIP SERVICE" OR LIFE'S SERVICE?

As children of God, we have the promise of salvation and are "set apart" through what the theologians call "sanctification." This brings us to the issue of "lip service" versus life's service. Do we "walk the walk" or just "talk the talk"? To examine this issue we will begin with the Master's words near the end of his Sermon on the Mount when he said:

> Not everyone who says to Me, "Lord, Lord," will enter the kingdom of heaven; but he who does the will of My Father who is in heaven. Many will say to Me on that [judgment] day, "Lord, Lord, did we not prophesy in Your name, and in Your name cast out demons, and in Your name perform many miracles?" And then I will declare to them, "I never knew you; depart from Me, you who practice lawlessness."
>
> Therefore everyone who hears these words of Mine, and acts upon them, may be compared to a wise man, who built his house upon the rock. And the rain

descended, and the floods came, and the winds blew, and burst against that house; and yet it did not fall, for it had been founded upon the rock. And everyone who hears these words of Mine, and does not act upon them, will be like a foolish man, who built his house upon the sand. And the rains descended and the floods came, and the winds blew, and burst against that house; and it fell, and great was its fall.[1]

In his epistle, James put this "actions speak louder than words" standard as follows:

What use is it, my brethren, if a man says he has faith, but he has no works? Can that faith save him? If a brother or sister is without clothing and in need of daily food, and one of you says to them, "Go in peace, be warmed and be filled", and yet you do not give them what is necessary for their body, what use is that? Even so faith, if it has no works, is dead, being by itself.

But someone may well say, "You have faith, and I have works; show me your faith without the works, and I will show you my faith by my works."[2]

This is not to promote salvation by works. We have dealt with that in Chapter 6, and we remember Paul's words:

For by grace you have been saved through faith; and that not of yourselves, it is the gift of God; not as a result of works, that no one should boast.[3]

This is to reiterate that the bridge of faith is built upon the foundation of God's grace; and our crossing is made plain by the change in our lives, which change itself is productive of the works about which James wrote.

Jesus used an illustration to remove any doubt about the matter. He spoke to the chief priests and the elders of the people during the week before his crucifixion. Mind you, now, they were the religious leaders of that day. He said to them:

> "What do you think? A man had two sons; and he went to the first and said, 'Son, go and work in the vineyard today.' And he answered, 'I will not'; but afterward he repented and went. And he went to the second and said the same; and he answered, 'I go, sir,' but did not go. Which of the two did the will of his father?" They said, "The first." Jesus said to them, "Truly, I say to you, the tax collectors and the harlots go into the kingdom of God before you. For John [the Baptist] came to you in the way of righteousness, and you did not believe him, but the tax collectors and the harlots believed him; and even when you saw it, you did not afterward repent and believe him.[4]

The point of the parable is not to commend tax collecting and harlotry, but to expose those who professed to be religious and yet ignored the way of righteousness preached to them by John the Baptist. It was Jesus' way of saying that actions speak louder than words.

Bearing these things in mind, we turn to the Scriptures to learn about the will of the "Father who is in heaven" that we might do his will while here on earth.

First, we take comfort in the Master's parable about the mustard seed.

> He presented another parable to them, saying, "The kingdom of heaven is like a mustard seed, which a man took and sowed in his field; and this is smaller than all other

seeds; but when it is full grown, it is larger than the garden plants, and becomes a tree, so that the birds of the air come and nest in its branches."[5]

This teaches us that at the beginning the Kingdom in our hearts may be as small as a mustard seed, but that it will grow to give us refuge, comfort, and peace. We shall consider how this may come about under rubrics of:

- The law and its spirit,
- The fruits of the Spirit,
- The influence of the Kingdom,
- The "fields white for harvest", and
- One more chance.

To understand and apply these teachings to our lives, we must have the help of the Holy Spirit. We are looking at spiritual standards, and we have already seen that they are beyond the comprehension of the natural man. However we are reassured by Jesus who, speaking at the Last Supper, said:

> If ye love me, keep my commandments. And I will pray the Father, and he shall give you another Comforter, that he may abide with you for ever; even the Spirit of truth; whom the world cannot receive, because it seeth him not, neither knoweth him: but ye know him; for he dwelleth with you, and shall be in you.[6]

He went on to tell them:

> But the Comforter, which is the Holy Ghost, whom the Father will send in my name, he shall teach you all things, and bring all things to your remembrance, whatsoever I have said unto you.[7]

And again, this time making clear that his Apostles were to be his witnesses to the truth:

> But when the Comforter is come, whom I will send unto you from the Father, even the Spirit of truth, which proceedeth from the Father, he shall testify of me: and ye also shall bear witness, because ye have been with me from the beginning.[8]

Still later he said:

> Howbeit when he, the Spirit of truth, is come, he will guide you into all truth: . . . [9]

Pentecost showed us that the Spirit came not to the Apostles only, but to all the Lord's followers. So we can trust that, if we seek and accept it, we shall have the guidance of the "Spirit of truth" in understanding these principles by which we are meant to live in this world.

THE LAW AND ITS SPIRIT

We have seen that the prophecies of Jeremiah and Ezekiel concerning the new covenant call for God's law to be written in the hearts of God's people. The writer of the letter to the Hebrews well understood this and quoted in that letter from Jeremiah's prophecy.[10] But we still live in a world where not all are believers. The laws are not written in the hearts of all people in today's society. So we need an external articulation of the law,—or we have anarchy, both legally and morally. Even though he came as the Messiah and will return as the King, Jesus told the people:

> Think not that I am come to destroy the law, or the prophets. I am not come to destroy, but to fulfill. For verily I

215

say unto you, till heaven and earth pass, one jot or one tittle shall in no wise pass from the law, till all be fulfilled. Whosoever therefore shall break one of these least commandments, and shall teach men so, he shall be called the least in the kingdom of heaven: but whosoever shall do and teach them, the same shall be called great in the kingdom of heaven.[11]

The new covenant was promised to the Jews; but Paul tells the Gentiles that the law can be written in their hearts, as well. To the Romans he wrote these words:

For it is not those who hear the law who are just in the sight of God; rather, those who observe the law will be justified. For when the Gentiles who do not have the law by nature observe the prescriptions of the law, they are a law for themselves even though they do not have the law. They show that the demands of the law are written in their hearts, while their conscience also bears witness and their conflicting thoughts accuse or even defend them on the day when, according to my gospel, God will judge people's hidden works through Christ Jesus.[12]

The law is our teacher as to what is right and what is wrong. That is, "by the law is the knowledge of sin".[13] So we can apply the law to facts and circumstances in our lives to produce justice and righteousness.

When Jesus came to fulfill the law he did so by revealing the spirit of the law, which is the spirit of love and service. The spirit of the law must touch the spirit of the man. Love must be his motivation if he obeys the spirit of the law and not its letter only. So Paul could describe himself as a servant of "a new covenant, not of the letter, but of the Spirit; for the letter kills, but the Spirit gives life."[14]

One example used by Jesus again and again was the Sabbath. He healed on the Sabbath. When he healed a man with a withered hand, he said to those who would accuse him of breaking the Sabbath, "Is it lawful to do good on the sabbath days, or to do evil? To save life, or to kill?"[15] He also healed on other sabbath days to the discomfiture of the Pharisees.[16] When they criticized him because his disciples ate corn as they walked through cornfields on the Sabbath, Jesus told them:

> The sabbath was made for man, and not man for the sabbath: Therefore the Son of man is Lord also of the sabbath.[17]

So we see then that the law of the Sabbath is not revoked or abandoned, but that it is to be observed for the right reasons and in the right way.

Jesus was critical of the religious leaders precisely because their strict and formalistic compliance with the law was in the wrong spirit. They keep the letter, and ignored the spirit of the law. He said:

> But woe to you Pharisees! For you pay tithe of mint and rue and every kind of garden herb, and yet disregard justice and the love of God; but these are the things you should have done without neglecting the others.[18]

And he said:

> . . . Woe to you lawyers as well! For you weigh men down with burdens hard to bear, while you yourselves will not even touch the burdens with one of your fingers.[19]

And he told his disciples:

> . . . Beware of the leaven of the Pharisees, which is hypocrisy.[20]

They were focused on the technicalities of the law, not its purpose. The law is to be used in the right spirit, the spirit of love and service. What one does is important; but of no less importance is why he does it. The motivation for one's action comes from his heart. As the Master said:

> A good man out of the good treasure of the heart bringeth forth good things; and an evil man out of the evil treasure bringeth forth evil things.[21]

While we consider the brain to be the seat of one's intellect and reason, the Bible speaks of one's "heart" as the very seat of life, the innermost spirit, the deepest part of one's emotional nature and understanding.[22] Therefore, to "get right with God" we need to open our hearts to the spirit of love and service, by which our actions will be motivated. Then, too, we will appreciate the Apostle's words:

> Owe no man any thing, but to love one another: for he that loveth another hath fulfilled the law.[23]

THE FRUITS OF THE SPIRIT

Once again we look to the parables by which Jesus taught his disciples and, likewise, teaches us. He told them the parable of the talents in which a man who was going on a journey left his money in the hands of his three servants. To one he gave five talents, to another two talents, and to a third one talent.[24] His purpose was that they use his money during his absence to make him a profit. Upon his return he called them in for an accounting. The one to whom he had given five talents had earned five more. The one to whom he had given two talents had earned two more. The master was pleased with both of them and gave them additional responsibilities. Now we read about the third servant:

> Then the one who had received the one talent came forward and said, "Master, I knew you were a demanding person, harvesting where you did not plant and gathering where you did not scatter; so out of fear I went off and buried your talent in the ground. Here it is back." His master said to him in reply, "You wicked, lazy servant! So you knew that I harvest where I did not plant and gather where I did not scatter? Should you not then have put my money in the bank so that I could have got it back with interest on my return? Now then! Take the talent from him and give it to the one with ten. For to everyone who has, more will be given and he will grow rich; but from the one who has not, even what he has will be taken away. And throw this useless servant into the darkness outside, where there will be wailing and grinding of teeth."[25]

Although Jesus himself did not explain this parable, it is interpreted as referring to his leaving us on earth after his Ascension and before his Second Coming. It tells us that we are to use the resources entrusted to us, for the glory of God. If we do so, we can expect rewards in the kingdom of heaven. This is not unlike what Jesus then taught about the Judgment, i.e., if we don't share with others of God's children, we shall be numbered among the goats on that Day.[26]

THE BRIDGE OF FAITH

We who inhabit this earth are people with needs. We also have various skills. We are users, and at the same time we are expected to be producers. God has graciously provided humankind with resources, such as:

- Time—for learning, for work, and for rest.
- Materials—such as land, minerals, water, plants, and animals.
- Intelligence—by the use of which men have developed a medium of exchange (money) and technology for communication, transportation, and production.
- Talents—which differ from person to person but which, all together, can be used to meet every material need.
- Energy—first muscle-power, but also wind, steam, electric and nuclear power.

All these resources are finite. That is, by their very nature, they are limited. Economics is the method by which limited resources are allocated, distributed, and used for the needs of people. But there are not enough resources to provide every person with every thing he wants; and, too often, not enough for the bare minimum of what he needs.

God has given it into our charge, both as individuals and as a community, to see that our time, material, and intellect are all used in a manner which is consistent with his will. That means in a manner which manifests love for God and love for other people. *We must recognize that our time, our talents and our other resources can be wasted, or simply used for our own selfish purposes. All of them should be used in God's service. It's our choice,—with consequences, responsibility, and accountability.* Jesus explains how we can do this. He said:

I am the true vine, and My Father is the vinedresser. Every branch in Me that does not bear fruit, He takes away; and every branch that bears fruit, He prunes it, that it may bear more fruit. . . . Abide in Me, and I in you. As the branch cannot bear fruit of itself, unless it abides in the vine, so neither can you, unless you abide in Me. I am the vine, you are the branches; he who abides in Me, and I in him, he bears much fruit; for apart from Me you can do nothing . . .

By this is My Father glorified, that you bear much fruit, and so prove to be My disciples.[27]

Paul described the fruits of the spirit. To the Galatians he spoke of love, joy, peace, longsuffering, gentleness, goodness, faith, meekness, and temperance.[28] He told the Ephesians "the fruit of the Spirit is in all goodness and righteousness and truth."[29]

THE INFLUENCE OF THE KINGDOM

The "fruits of the Spirit" lead us to a short parable told by the Master:

He spoke another parable to them, "The kingdom of heaven is like leaven, which a woman took, and hid in three pecks of meal, until it was all leavened."[30]

The point here is that, while we wait for his Second Coming, the children of God are to be an influence in the world. As individuals, each of us is responsible for his influence in his group or community. Each is accountable for the group's misuse of resources, if his influence could have prevented such misuse.

We are to serve as God's hands on earth—to carry out his will and for his glory. We are to serve as God's feet—running to serve the needs of those who call upon him for help. To use the Master's metaphors: We are to be the salt of the earth,[31] the light of the world,[32] and aqueducts of living water.[33] We must see then that the salt does not lose its savor,[34] and that the light be not hid "under a bushel."[35] We must likewise see that our attitudes and actions do not dam up these aqueducts of living waters.

One more metaphor: if we are to be candles and bring light to others, it is only as the Holy Spirit is the flame. Our lives are to be the wicks, our resources the wax. The wick will be lit by the Spirit and the wax will furnish fuel to bring light to others in this sin-darkened world.

Our Christian responsibility to be examples for others is a serious responsibility; and we cannot just go our own way, oblivious to the temptations we may set before others by careless words or behavior.

Jesus said to his disciples, "Occasions for stumbling are bound to come, but woe to anyone by whom they come! It would be better for you if a millstone were hung around your neck and you were thrown into the sea than for you to cause one of these little ones to stumble. . ."[36]

"FIELDS WHITE FOR HARVEST"

Jesus spoke of evangelism as reaping the harvest. For example, he spoke to his disciples, saying:

Do you not say, "There are yet four months, and then comes the harvest"? Behold, I say to you, lift up your eyes, and look on the fields, that they are white for harvest. Already he who reaps is receiving wages, and is gathering fruit for life eternal; that he who sows and he who reaps may rejoice together. For in this case the saying is true, "One sows, and another reaps."

I sent you to reap that for which you have not labored; others have labored, and you have entered into their labor.[37]

When he sent out the seventy before him he said to them:

The harvest is plentiful, but the laborers are few; therefore beseech the Lord of the harvest to send out laborers into His harvest.[38]

These instructions to his disciples suggest that all of us should be "fishers of men,"[39] as he told Simon and Andrew they would be. It is by these instructions that evangelistic Christians are motivated to harvest the fields and fish the streams for converts, who shall become children of God. They take seriously the "Great Commission":

Go ye into all the world, and preach the gospel to every creature. He that believeth and is baptized shall be saved; but he that believeth not shall be damned.[40]

While it is true that each of us must make his own decision, we remember:

For whosoever shall call upon the name of the Lord shall be saved. How then shall they call on him in whom they have not believed? and how shall they believe in him of whom they have not heard? and how shall they hear without a preacher? and how shall they preach, except they be sent? As it is written, "How beautiful are the feet of them that preach the gospel of peace, and bring glad tidings of good things!"[41]

Finally, we turn to another parable related to the harvest. This one makes two points in connection with our subject here, which Jesus didn't explain but which we can see upon reflection. First, the parable:

> And he said, "So is the kingdom of God, as if a man should cast seed into the ground; and should sleep, and rise night and day, and the seed should spring and grow up, he knoweth not how. For the earth bringeth forth fruit of herself; first the blade, then the ear, after that the full corn in the ear. But when the fruit is brought forth, immediately he putteth in the sickle, because the harvest is come."[42]

Comparing this parable with the Master's words reported by John,[43] we see that our duties as Christians are (1) to sow by word and example, and (2) to reap by evangelism. Others may attend the conversion of those to whom we have been an influence, and vice versa. In this context, not everybody reaps what he sows, or sows what he reaps. In any event, the Spirit of God must bless our efforts if there are to be good results.[44] This is another way of understanding the parable to mean that our work for the Kingdom can bring forth good fruits, even if we don't know how they grow.

ONE MORE CHANCE

As we have seen elsewhere, we do not know when our Lord is coming again. Neither do we know when our lives on earth will end. But we have an illustration of God's patience.

And he began telling this parable:

"A certain man had a fig tree which had been planted in his vineyard; and he came looking for fruit on it, and did not find any. And he said to the vineyard keeper, 'Behold, for three years I have come looking for fruit on this fig tree without finding any. Cut it down! Why does it even use up the ground?' And he answered and said to him, 'Let it alone, sir, for this year too, until I dig around it and put in fertilizer; and if it bears fruit next year, fine; but if not, cut it down.'"[45]

This tells us plainly that God has patience, but patience has limits. The fig tree was given one more chance to bear fruit. If we heed this parable and its lesson, we will take advantage of the "one more chance" we are given to bear fruit. Then we shall hear at the Judgment those welcome words: "Well done, thou good and faithful servant; . . . enter thou into the joy of thy Lord."[46]

CONCLUSIONS

T his book is not easy reading. As my youngest daughter will say, "Dad, this is no 'Dick and Jane.'" I make no apology for that, because those who have come this far will have given some thoughtful consideration to the premises of Christianity—to *why* "The Spirit and the bride say, 'Come.'"[1] The subject merits thoughtful consideration. Nothing less. After all, what could be of greater significance to any person than the Creator's claims on his life? What could be more important to him than the promises concerning his eternal destiny?

Those who have given the matter thoughtful consideration and still do not understand may nevertheless take heart. The gospel does not require understanding. It requires only *belief*. Even the Apostle Paul did not fully understand, so he said:

For we know in part, and we prophesy in part; but when the perfect comes, the partial will be done away. . . . For

now we see in a mirror dimly, but then face to face; now
I know in part, but then I shall know fully just as I also
have been fully known.[2]

Spiritual things are not intellectually understood, but spiritually perceived.[3]

Therefore, the thesis here has been to invite attention
to the premises for the Christian gospel, and its invitation
to cross the bridge of faith under a white flag—surrendering time, talents, energy, and resources to the power and
the purposes of God.

Of course this book does not exhaust the subject. The
subject is so vast that nobody can deal with the whole.
McGrath tells this story:

> . . . Once upon a time, Augustine of Hippo, a celebrated
> theologian, was writing a work on the Trinity, exploring
> the Christian understanding of God. As he was walking
> along the coast one day, he encountered a small boy pouring seawater into a hole in the ground. Augustine
> watched him for some time, and eventually asked him
> what he was doing. "I'm pouring the Mediterranean Sea
> into this hole," replied the boy.
>
> "Don't be so stupid," replied Augustine, "You can't
> fit the sea into that little hole. You're wasting your time."
>
> "And so are you," replied the boy, "trying to write a
> book about God."[4]

The Bible is now available in many different translations. Some Bibles are leather-bound; some "hard-bound";
and some paperback. They can be found in large print or in
audio. Many have commentaries and concordances. They
may differ in form, but all of them still teach creation, the
Ten Commandments, sin, salvation, and access by faith to
the kingdom of God. The Bible still teaches that we are to

love God and to love each other. It still tells of the grace of God and describes the fruits of the Spirit. The revelation of God through the written Word has not been eroded, erased or changed by the passage of time. Science and technology have not made the Bible obsolete. Neither has the modern theological academy done so. The Bible still speaks truth.

Now, I know that during the last 150 years historical criticism by theologians has brought doubt to the minds of many people. Bishop Spong wrote: "The Bible is full of contradictions."[5] He scoffs at the "naive literalism of the fundamentalists"[6] and says, "fundamentalist Christians distort the Bible by taking it literally."[7]

My problem with Bishop Spong and others who use "scientific" methods to interpret the Bible is their use of a methodology appropriate for the material world but inappropriate for the kingdom of God. There is a difference between what is true in a material sense, i.e., fact as happening in time and space, and true in a spiritual sense, i.e., the transcendent, in which the opinions of men are not determinative. Men can observe the first, and scientists can design methods by which they try to test such matters. Rationalists cannot reach spiritual truth. God must reveal it to those who accept his revelation in faith.

If that premise be true, as I believe it to be, then the scientists who will not believe in miracles will not believe much of the Bible. Believers agree that God uses men to do his work on earth. Men are fallible. God knows that. If he chose to use fallible men to write the books we now refer to collectively as the Bible, the question is did they mess it up or is it inerrant in every way essential to our relationship with God.

The answer to that question depends on one's presupposition as to the purpose of God in having men write the books of the Bible. If his purpose was to reveal his nature and character to those whom he created, we can surely believe that those parts of the Scriptures that deal with spiritual truth may be accepted as true. And this is so even though fallible men may have contradicted each other as to some matters of fact.

Bearing these things in mind, I have tried to ground this book upon the Bible, insofar as the Spirit of Truth has given me light to understand it. Because the Bible uses parables, examples, and metaphors to explain spiritual truths, there is room for honest differences in interpretation. Any writer must concede that. Of course, I do. Even so, any writer who tries to light a candle in a world of spiritual darkness must do so believing that the Spirit will help his readers to see by whatever light is available. I pray that he will do so for every person who reads this book.

At the outset, I said that the purpose of this book is to examine the essential premises upon which Christianity rests. Parents need to explain these fundamentals to their children, and believers sometimes find themselves defending their faith to others. This book is my effort to help them do so; not in a theologian's terms, but in words which laypeople can grasp. My aim has been to deal with the fundamentals, the essentials.

So what are the essentials we have tried to examine?

First, there are some beliefs which, although widely held, are *not the essentials* of Christianity. They should not divert attention from the essentials. Christians differ as to church government or polity. They differ as to use of liturgy and icons. Many believe that priests have special access to God; many disagree. Some feel driven to handling snakes.[8] There are charismatics who believe that the Spirit lives only in those who speak in tongues.[9] There are other differences, too many to mention here. Many Christians seem to thrive on theological debates. I feel bold to assert that of these examples none is essential to a relationship to God through Jesus Christ.

On the other hand, I do believe the following premises to be essential to the Christian faith:

- The creation of the heavens, the earth, and humankind by a God of purpose;
- The revelation to man of God's own spiritual attributes, such as love, truth, righteousness, justice and mercy;
- The revelation to man of God's law, which provides standards of behavior and values by which people can live together in a family or community;
- Man's God-given freedom of choice, with accountability for sin;
- Mankind's sinful self-centeredness, in spite of God's worthiness of worship and obedience;
- Jesus of Nazareth is the incarnate revelation of the nature and character of God, himself a spirit;
- The provision, through God's own love and grace, of Jesus as "the Lamb of God that taketh away the sin of the world", by his crucifixion, death and resurrection;
- The need for repentance and faith to bridge the gulf between the self-centered sin of man and the kingdom of God;
- The Holy Spirit as the influence of God which convicts man of sin, provides the light of truth for man's guidance, and strengthens man in serving God's will and purpose; and
- A new birth of man's spirit into the kingdom of God on earth, with the promise of eternal life in the presence of God.

We are unfinished people. Each of us has a yearning for something or someone outside himself. Some try to satisfy this need with a friend, a spouse, or a sweetheart. Others try to satisfy it with position, status, or "respect." Still others seek power and money. The only true satisfaction is in God. The joy of "full-time Christian service" is not reserved to missionaries, pastors, and their paid staff. God's purpose for you and me may be secular, but it becomes sacred when done in his name and for his glory. You may be called to be a farmer, a schoolteacher, or a secretary. You may have the talent and opportunity to be an artist, a nurse, or a carpenter. These and countless other vocations are honorable and needed in communities such as ours. God's purpose is served when a secular vocation, business or profession meets a legitimate need and does so honestly and fairly, in a loving spirit.

We live in a land and a generation that seem to focus on "rights" and, at the same time, to misunderstand their relation to responsibilities. The greatest of the human rights is freedom of choice; but not all choices are equal, not all choices are right, not all choices are honorable, and not all choices are fair. With freedom to choose between right and wrong comes the awesome responsibility to bear the consequences of choosing the wrong. Life's most significant choice is whether one will cross the bridge of faith, or decline the invitation to do so and thereby exclude himself from the kingdom of God.

The natural man is motivated by his "primal urges" or appetites such as hunger, thirst, sleep, sex, avarice, intemperance, and self-preservation. He is also motivated by his emotions, which can lead him to embrace pride and to crave approval by others, even when their approval requires bad behavior. So likewise he can be motivated by his intellect, through which he tries to define rational goals with rational means and strategic planning. His conscience responds to training in religious, philosophical, moral and ethical values as well as to his own intuitive standards of right and wrong. All these, singly or together, serve as the motivating forces for a person's actions.

Those who have been born again of the spirit of God embrace the Holy Spirit as their motivator, believing that he will give them the light of truth as well as encouragement in their love for God and neighbor. For them the goal must be right,—God's purpose. For them the reasons must be right,—God's glory. For them the means must be right,—God's law in spirit and in truth. This rebirth in the spirit does not remove the physical needs or appetites. Neither does it destroy intellect or emotion. But it remolds all of these motivators, under the guidance of the Holy Spirit of God.

Here a word to believers and inquirers about the unbelieving rationalists, humanists, and scoffers. Neither their attitudes nor their harangues are new. Satan, the father of lies, uses doubt in his efforts to undermine faith. Don't be afraid of them, and don't be misled. On the contrary, consider a paraphrase of the "Pascal Wager." Either the bridge of faith leads from sin and death to the kingdom of God, or it doesn't. If you wager that it does, and it *does*, then you will have gained access to the kingdom of God. If it does not, you will have lost little. On the other hand, if you bet that the bridge of faith leads nowhere, and in fact it leads to the kingdom of God, you will have lost eternal life by your bad bet.

God is spirit, but not just a bundle of inchoate characteristics or attributes of character. As revealed to Israel by the Old Testament Pentateuch, the patriarchs and the prophets, the Creator is a person of infinite power and perfect purpose. He has an identity, a self, and a personality. He is the indescribable One; but we know him by evidence of his inexhaustible grace and everlasting love. We tend to anthropomorphize God, speaking or thinking of him as a likeness of us. We speak of the "hand" of God as if he were physical. Not so. But neither is God an "it" without the capacity for wisdom, power and love. We have a fuller revelation of God's person, nature and character in the New Testament, where we are told that this spirit of God for a time became man.

At Christmas time we speak of Jesus as the Prince of Peace; and many people think that he will bring reconciliation and an absence of hostility between the men and nations of this earth. On the contrary, he himself said that there would be "wars and rumors of wars",[10] because "nation shall rise against nation, and kingdom against kingdom".[11] Until the Second Coming, the peace he brings is peace of mind and heart from the God of peace.[12]

One who is a born-again Christian has that peace. Moreover, he is:

- No longer afraid of life—or death—but confident in the promises of God;
- No longer lonely, but always aware of the presence of the Spirit of God;
- No longer thirsty for a purpose in life, but filled with living waters flowing through himself to serve the needs of others;
- No longer dead in sin, but alive in the spirit of truth and love and righteousness;
- No longer a slave to Satan and self, but free to serve and worship the living God; and

- No longer living in worry, doubt and fear, but joyfully trusting in the Creator for all the needs of the body as well as the needs of the spirit.

Having made it to the last pages of this book, I pray that you will ask, "How do I walk across the bridge of faith?" The answer is that, *believing these essentials,* each of us can make this prayer:

Almighty Creator and everliving God:
I have been self-centered,
instead of focused on you.
I've disobeyed your law,
in both letter and spirit.
I have come far short of my potential
in the purpose you have for my life.
I've missed opportunities to be kind,
and chances to help those who've needed help.
I have not loved others;
and I've been unforgiving.
I have sinned in these, and in many other ways.
I confess that I have only myself to blame.
Here and now, I repent and choose
to turn my life over to you and to your purposes.
I pledge my time, talents, energy, and resources to
your service.
All this I do because I believe that Jesus Christ died for me, as the Lamb slain to seal your new covenant with mankind;
And relying on your grace and mercy for my salvation, I confess him to be my Lord and Savior.
Amen.

This prayer, made in sincerity and honestly, will bring one onto the bridge of faith, which is founded on the grace of God and leads to the kingdom of God. This prayer should be followed by a *public* confession of faith[13] and then baptism.[14]

Baptism tells the world that you have made your own personal decision, that you have repented, that you believe, and that you take Jesus Christ as your Savior and Lord. By baptism, you take a public stand and an identity by which you are prepared to live. Through baptism you are initiated into the Church Universal, the kingdom of God on earth. You become a part of the company of the committed and can share in its work.

Your choice of a denomination and a particular local church will depend on many things, including your own religious background and upbringing, your acceptance of its theology, and your compatibility with its congregation and its culture. All of these should be carefully considered before your choice is made. Then when a congenial church is identified, join it to be of service to your Lord through the opportunities the church affords.

With that last advice, I leave you with this prayer:

Now the God of peace, that brought again from the dead our Lord Jesus, that great shepherd of the sheep, through the blood of the everlasting covenant, make you perfect in every good work to do his will, working in you that which is well-pleasing in his sight, through Jesus Christ; to whom be glory for ever and ever. Amen.[15]

Notes

FOREWORD

1. John 16:13. All references are to the King James Version unless otherwise noted.
2. Luke 9:23–24. See also Matthew 16:24–25 and Mark 8:34–35.
3. Just as our understanding of God is limited, so likewise limited is our means of referring to God. In English we have gender pronouns only for male, female, or neuter, i.e., he, she, or it. To call God "It" would depersonalize God, and that would be insulting. God created male and female, but God is beyond gender, so our language has no pronoun fit for God. To call God "She" is nothing more nor less than to mollify feminists and thereby be "politically correct" at the expense of reality. So I shall continue a practice which was acceptable from the time of the first translation into English of Hebrew, Aramaic and Greek references to the Creator. Even though I believe that God has no masculine gender, I shall use the masculine pronouns.

   Moreover, I shall follow the example of John L. Locke in *The De-Voicing of Society*, (NY: Simon & Schuster, 1998, page 16), where he included a note to readers in the following language, "To avoid awkwardness of expression, I have used 'he', 'him', and 'his' in a few places where pronouns of either gender would be appropriate. No disrespect is intended toward female readers".

CHAPTER ONE

1. James S. Trefil, *Space Time Infinity*, (Washington: Smithsonian Books, 1985) page 10.
2. Ibid., pages 10–11.
3. *The American Heritage Dictionary*, Second College Edition, (Boston: Houghton Mifflin Co., 1991).
4. Ibid.
5. Ibid.
6. Ibid.
7. Ibid.
8. Ibid.
9. Ibid.
10. George MacDonald , *A Dish of Orts*, (London: Sampson Low, Marston & Co., 1893, 1895, re-published 1996 by Johannesen, Whitethorn, CA) p. 11.
11. Brian L. Silver, *The Ascent of Science*, (NY: Oxford University Press, 1998), page 339.
12. Gen. 1:1.
13. Gen. 1:27.
14. Silver, op. cit., page 464.
15. John 4:24.
16. Matt. 18:3.
17. Gen. 1:1; Ex. 20:11; Deut. 4:32.
18. Ps. 8:1–9; 102:25; 104:1–30; 148:5.
19. Eccl. 12:1; Isa. 40:25–26, 28; 42:5; Jer. 31:35; Mal. 2:10.
20. Mark 10:6; 13:19.
21. Margaret Nutting Ralph, *"And God Said What?"*, (Mahwah, NJ: Paulist Press, 1986), page 30.
22. Ibid.
23. Stanley J. Grenz, *Created for Community*, 2d. Ed., (Grand Rapids, MI: Baker Books, 1998), pages 165–168.
24. John Dominic Crossan, *Jesus: A Revolutionary Biography*, (San Francisco: Harper, 1995), pages 82, 95, 160–161.
25. See Matt. 13:10–17; 34–35; Mark 4:10–12, 34; Lk. 8:9–10; John 16:25–30.
26. I Cor. 7:17 (NRSV).
27. Rom. 9:10–12.
28. Ex. 9:16; Rom. 9:17.
29. Dan. 2:37–38.
30. John 12:27; 18:37; Eph. 3:11; I John 3:8.

31. Eph. 1:3–12.
32. Eph. 1:13–14.
33. Eph. 1:3–11 (NRSV).
34. II Tim. 1:8–9 (NRSV).
35. Rom. 8:28 (NRSV).
36. Gen. 50:20.
37. I Cor. 12:18 (NRSV).
38. Oswald Chambers, *My Utmost for His Highest*, (Uhrichsville, OH: Barbour and Company, Inc., Christian Library Edition, 1991), page 249.

CHAPTER TWO

1. Karl Barth, *The Humanity of God*, (Richmond, VA: John Knox Press, 1960).
2. Gen. 1:27.
3. Deut. 30:19 (NASB).
4. Sir. 15:14–17 (The New American Bible, hereinafter "NAB").
5. T. Kermit Scott, *Augustine: His Thought in Context*, (Mahwah, New Jersey: Paulist Press, 1995), pages 158–159.
6. Barth, op. cit., p. 75.
7. Barth, op. cit., p. 77.
8. Rom. 1:20–23. (NASB) Parenthetical added.
9. Carl F. H. Henry, Editor, *Fundamentals of the Faith*, (Grand Rapids, MI: Zondervan Publishing House, 1969), page 121.
10. G. K. Chesterton, *Orthodoxy*, (NY: Doubleday, 1990), page 78.
11. Ibid., pages 136–137.
12. See William J. Bennett, *The Death of Outrage*, (NY: The Free Press, A Division of Simon & Schuster, 1998).
13. II Pet. 3:15–16.
14. Rom. 1:18–19, 24–26 (RSV).
15. Jer. 31:31–33.
16. Ezek. 36:26–27.
17. II Cor. 3:5–6.
18. Rom. 5:1.
19. I Cor. 6:12.
20. I Cor. 10:23.
21. Gal. 5:13–14.
22. Rom. 13:8.
23. Ps. 81:11–16 (NASB).
24. Chesterton, op. cit., page 137.

25. Josh. 24:15.
26. Barth, op. cit., page 82.

CHAPTER THREE

1. Harold S. Kushner, *When Bad Things Happen to Good People*, (NY: Avon Books, 1983), pages 80–81. From *When Bad Things Happen to Good People* by Harold S. Kushner. Copyright © 1981, 1989 by Harold S. Kushner. Reprinted by permission of Schocken Books, a division of Random House, Inc.
2. *HarperCollins Study Bible* (NY: HarperCollins, 1993) Introduction to the book of Job, page 749.
3. Gal. 6:7–8.
4. Ezk. 16:43.
5. Heb. 12:5–11; Ps. 38; Ezk. 17:18–19.
6. John 9:1–41; 11:4.
7. Jas. 1:2–4; I Peter 1:6–9; Job 36:15, 21–23.
8. II Cor. 1:3–6.
9. John 15:12, 17.
10. John 15:1–2; Luke 13:1–9.
11. Rom. 5:3–5.
12. Kushner, op. cit., pages 38–39.
13. Ibid., pages 46, 53.
14. Job 38:4 (NASB).
15. Job 38:12 (NASB).
16. Job 38:19 (NASB).
17. Job 38:31 (NASB).
18. Job 38:36 (NASB).
19. Job 39:26–27 (NASB).
20. George MacDonald , *Unspoken Sermons, Series II*, (London: Longmans, Green & Co., 1885; type-copied by Johannesen, 1997), pages 352–353.
21. Ibid., page 360.
22. Job 1:1.
23. Job 1:8–12, 2:3–6.
24. Luke 22:3–6; Rev. 2:9–10.
25. Rom. 8:35–39 (NASB).
26. Rom. 5:3–5.
27. Matt. 5:10.
28. Matt. 5:11.

29. Matt. 6:19.
30. Matt. 5:44.
31. Matt. 10:36.
32. Rom. 8:28. (NASB)
33. Bernie S. Siegel, M.D., *Love, Medicine & Miracles*, (NY: Harper & Row, Perennial Library Ed., 1988), page 214.

CHAPTER FOUR

1. Rom. 3:23, Emphasis added.
2. I John 1:8.
3. In an article following several school-site killings, "experts" spoke of the young killers as "outsiders", "kids who were out of the mainstream—unhappy, searching for their place, and suffering ridicule." One psychiatrist was said to have pointed out "that virtually all of these violent children feel no one cares about them." See *U. S. News & World Report*, June 1, 1998, pages 17–18. As we shall see, self-centeredness is the fertile ground for sin; and these are self-centered young people who are frustrated when others refuse to make them the focus of attention. Their self-centeredness may help to explain their actions, but it does not excuse them.
4. Karl Menninger, M.D., *Whatever Became of Sin?*, (NY: Hawthorn Books, Inc., 1973), page 46.
5. Ibid., page 48.
6. Luke 14:26. Cf. Matt. 19:29; Mark 10:29–30.
7. Matt. 12:46–50. Cf. Mark 3:31–35; Luke 8:19–21.
8. Alister E. McGrath, *Studies in Doctrine*, (Grand Rapids, MI: Zondervan Publishing House, 1997), page 369.
9. Ted Peters, *Sin: Radical Evil in Soul and Society*, (Grand Rapids, MI: William B. Eerdmans Publishing Company, 1994), page 7.
10. Ibid., page 8.
11. Wayne Gruden, *Systematic Theology*, (Grand Rapids, MI: Zondervan Publishing House, 1994), page 490.
12. St. Augustine, *The Confessions*, with Introduction, Translation and Notes by Maria Boulding, O.P. B., (Hyde Park, NY: New City Press, 1997).
13. McGrath, op. cit., pages 376, et seq.
14. See Menninger, op. cit., pages 226–227, where he speaks of egocentricity and quotes at length from Arnold Toynbee, *Surviving the Future*, (Oxford University Press, 1971).

15. Owen Chadwick, *A History of Christianity*, (NY: St. Martin's Press, 1995), page 126.
16. Peters, *Sin*, op. cit., pages 7–8.
17. C. S. Lewis, *Mere Christianity*, (NY: Simon & Schuster, First Touchstone Edition, 1996), pages 109–111. *Mere Christianity* by C.S. Lewis copyright © C.S. Lewis Pte. Ltd. 1942, 1943, 1944, 1952. Extracts reprinted by permission.
18. Matt. 6:15. And see Mark 11:26.
19. *Catechism of the Catholic Church*, (NY: Doubleday, an Image Book, 1995) Section 1866, page 509, lists the seven "capital sins" as pride, avarice, envy, wrath, lust, gluttony, and sloth or acedia.
20. Oswald Chambers, op. cit., page 206.
21. Herschel H. Hobbs, *What Baptists Believe*, (Nashville: Broadman Press, 1964), page 69.
22. John 8:34. Cf. Rom. 6:16.
23. *Catechism*, op. cit., Section 1850, page 505.
24. Matt. 25:31–46.
25. Ibid., verse 46.
26. Mark 10:24. See also Matt. 19:16–24; Luke 18:18–25.
27. Luke 6:24, emphasis added.
28. Luke 6:20. And see James 2:5.
29. Luke 12:48.
30. I John 3:17 (NRSV).
31. Rom. 6:23 (NASB).
32. Heb. 9:27 (NASB).
33. I Cor. 10:13.

CHAPTER FIVE

1. Owen Chadwick, op. cit., page 239.
2. Ibid.
3. This is Aramaic and means "empty head" or "good for nothing". (NASB note)
4. Matt. 5:21–22. (NASB)
5. Matt. 5:29–30. (NASB)
6. Luke 12:4–5. (NASB)
7. Matt. 23:33. (NASB)
8. Matt. 3:12. (NASB)
9. Matt. 7:19. (NASB) Compare with Matt. 3:8–12.
10. Matt. 13:49–50. (NASB) And see Matt. 13:41–43.
11. Mark 9:43. (NASB)

12. Rev. 20:14–15, 21:8. (NASB)
13. II Thes. 1:8–9 (RSV).
14. Gal. 5:22–23.
15. II Pet. 3:9. See also John 3:16 and I Tim. 2:1–6.
16. C. S. Lewis, *The Problem of Pain*, (NY: Simon & Schuster, First Touchstone Edition, 1996) pages 106–107. *The Problem of Pain* by C.S. Lewis copyright © C.S. Lewis Pte. Ltd. 1940. Extracts reprinted by permission.
17. Ibid., p. 111.
18. Ps. 98:9. (NASB)
19. Matt. 25:31–34. (NASB)
20. Matt. 25:41, 46. (NASB)
21. C. S. Lewis, *The Great Divorce*, (NY: Simon & Schuster, First Touchstone Edition, 1996), p. 118. *The Great Divorce* by C.S. Lewis copyright © C.S. Lewis Pte. Ltd. 1945. Extracts reprinted by permission.
22. Ibid., p. 72.
23. Matt. 16:24 (NASB); Mark 8:34; Luke 9:23.
24. John 12:27. (NASB)
25. John 13:34. (NASB)
26. Acts 9:4. (NASB)
27. Matt. 18:21–22. (NASB).

CHAPTER SIX

1. John 8:34.
2. James 1:14–15.
3. I John 4:8.
4. John 3:16.
5. See Acts 2:37–39 and I Cor. 14:24–25.
6. I John 4:19.
7. John 1:10.
8. John 17:14.
9. Luke 4:5–8; John 16:7–11.
10. John 8:3–11.
11. Matt. 23:27–33.
12. C. S. Lewis, *The Problem of Pain*, (NY: Simon & Schuster, Inc., First Touchstone Edition, 1996), page 33.
13. Eph. 2:5, 8–9; II Tim. 1:9.
14. Tit. 2:11.
15. Rom. 3:21–22, 24 (NAB).
16. Tit. 3:4–7 (NAB).

17. Rom. 3:24–26 (NAB), emphasis added.
18. Tit. 2:11–14.
19. II Cor. 8:9.
20. John 1:14, 17.
21. Acts 15:11.
22. Heb. 11:6 (NRSV).
23. John 20:6–9 (NAB), emphasis added.
24. Mark 10:14–15; Luke 18:16–17.
25. Luke 24:44–48, emphasis added.
26. I Cor. 2:1–5, 14 (NAB).
27. I Cor. 2:14.
28. I Cor. 1:20.
29. By "the foolishness of our proclamation", Paul refers to his own preaching. He calls the gospel "the power of God and the wisdom of God."
30. I Cor. 1:21–25 (NRSV), emphasis added.
31. Heb. 11:3 (NASB).
32. Acts 22:15.
33. Luke 24:48; Acts 1:8.
34. II Peter 1:16.
35. Luke 1:2.
36. Alexander Cruden, *Cruden's Complete Concordance to the Old and New Testaments*, edited by A. D. Adams, et al. (Philadelphia: The John C. Winston Company, 1949), page 754.
37. II Peter 1:16–18.
38. I John 1:1, 3 (RSV).
39. Matt. 10:38–39; Matt. 16:24–26; Mark 8:34–37; Luke 9:23–25; Luke 17:33; John 12:25–26.
40. Mark 1:15; Matt. 4:17; Luke 13:3.
41. Isa. 12:1–2; Matt. 12:21; Rom. 15:12; II Cor. 1:9–10; II Cor. 4:13–14; Eph. 1:12–13.
42. Heb. 12:22–24.
43. Jno. 3:16; Mark 1:14–15.
44. John 15:10.
45. John 13:34–35; John 15:12.
46. Luke 22:25–26; John 13:3–17.
47. Josh. 24:15 (NASB).
48. Melvin E. Dieter, et al., *Five Views on Sanctification*, (Grand Rapids, MI: Zondervan Publishing House, 1987).
49. See Job 42:1–6.

50. James 2:14–18 (NASB).
51. John 15:12.
52. I Cor. 12:12–13, 27.
53. John 15:1–8.
54. Cf. John 7:16–17.
55. Gen. 50:15–21.
56. Ex. 32:1–14.
57. Ex. 32:30–34.
58. I Kings 8:1–61; II Chron. 6:1–42.
59. II Chron. 7:12–15.
60. Jer. 31:31–34. See also Jer. 36:1–4.
61. Dan. 9:1–5, 16–19.
62. Luke 7:38.
63. Luke 7:47–50.
64. I John 1:9.
65. I John 2:12.
66. Acts 5:29–32.
67. Acts 13:38–39.
68. Acts 26:16–18.
69. Matt. 6:12.
70. Matt. 6:14–15. See also Mark 11:25–26.
71. Matt. 18:21–22.
72. Matt. 18:35.
73. Luke 6:37.
74. Luke 23:34.
75. Luke 13:3, emphasis added.
76. Luke 13:5, emphasis added.
77. Matt. 4:17 (NASB), emphasis added.
78. Acts 17:30–31.
79. Acts 26:20 (NASB).
80. Matt. 3:8–9 (RSV); Luke 3:8.
81. Luke 17:3–4 (NAB), emphasis added.
82. Rom. 12:17, 19 (NRSV).
83. II Pet. 3:9.
84. John 3:16.
85. Dietrich Bonhoeffer, *The Cost of Discipleship*, (NY: Collier Books of Macmillan Publishing Company, 1963), page 45.
86. Ibid., page 47.

CHAPTER SEVEN

1. Deut. 4:35.
2. Deut. 6:4.
3. Phylacteries are small boxes in which very small quotations of Scripture are deposited and which are worn on the arms and foreheads of some Jews. This practice is in accord with Deuteronomy 6:8.
4. See Deut. 6:9.
5. Bruce M. Metzger and Michael D. Coogan, Editors, *The Oxford Companion to the Bible*, (NY: Oxford University Press, 1993) pages 692–693.
6. II Kings 19:15; Isa. 37:16.
7. Isa. 43:10–11. To like effect, see Isa. 44:6, 24; Isa. 45:5, 6, 18, 21, 22; Isa. 46:9.
8. *The Quràn*, Eighth U. S. Ed., Tahrike Tarsile Quràn, Inc., Elmhurst, N.Y. (1993), 5:72.
9. Ibid., 5:73.
10. Ibid., 5:75.
11. Ibid., 2:163.
12. Thomas W. Lippman, *Understanding Islam*, Revised Edition, (NY: A Mentor Book, Penguin Group, 1990), page 8.
13. Deut. 6:4–5. See ft. 2, supra.
14. The scribe's quotation we have also seen above. Deut. 4:35. See ft. 1, supra.
15. The whole passage is from Mark 12:28–34. (NASB)
16. John 8:58–59. See also John 5:18 and John 10:33.
17. John 10:30 (RSV).
18. John 10:31–33, 39 (RSV), emphasis added.
19. Mark 14:61–62. And see Luke 22:67–70; Matt. 26:63–65.
20. Matt. 26:65–66; Mark 14:63–64.
21. Mark 3:5.
22. John 11:35–38.
23. Matt. 4:2; Luke 4:2.
24. John 19:28.
25. John 4:6.
26. Matt. 4:1–11; Mark 1:12–13; Luke 4:1–13.
27. Heb. 4:14–15.
28. Luke 4:22. And see Matt. 13:55–56; Mark 6:3; John 6:42.
29. Matt. 13:57; Mark 6:3.
30. Luke 4:28–30.

31. Matt. 13:58.
32. John 7:5.
33. Mark 3:20–21 (NASB).
34. Luke 4:16–21.
35. I Tim. 1:1 (RSV).
36. I Tim. 2:5–6 (RSV), emphasis added.
37. I Cor. 15:22–24 (RSV). Explanation inserted.
38. I Cor. 8:6 (RSV).
39. John 14:15–20, emphasis added.
40. John 14:9.
41. John 4:24.
42. McGrath, op. cit., pages 208–209.
43. Gen. 1:2.
44. Exod. 31:3, 35:31.
45. Num. 24:3.
46. I Sam. 10:10; 11:6; 19:23.
47. I Sam. 19:20; II Chron. 15:1.
48. Job 33:4.
49. Ezek. 11:24–25.
50. John 3:7.
51. John 7:37–39 (NAB).
52. Rev. 22:1.
53. Matt. 17:20 (NAB).
54. I Cor. 2:14.
55. John 7:16–17.
56. George MacDonald , *Hope of the Gospel*, as quoted in *3,000 Quotations from the Writings of George MacDonald* , Harry Verploegh, Compiler, (Grand Rapids, MI: Fleming H. Revell, 1996), p. 170.
57. J. B. Phillips, *Your God is Too Small*, (NY: The Macmillan Company, 1953) page 89.
58. John 14:6.
59. John 3:16.
60. John 12:27; and see John 18:37.
61. John 1:29.
62. Gal. 3:13–14.
63. Acts 13:23–26.
64. Of course, Jews deny the resurrection and some still await the Messiah. Rabbi Roy A. Rosenberg, *The Concise Guide to Judaism*, (NY: Mentor, Penguin Books, USA, Inc., 1991), pages 62–64, 231 et seq. While Islam teaches that Jesus was born of a virgin (Quràn

3:45–47; 19:16–21) it denies the crucifixion and resurrection, saying that God "took him up to Himself". (Quràn 4:157–158; 3:55)
See also Thomas W. Lippman, op. cit., pages 8, 121.
65. Matt. 12:38–40; Luke 11:16, 29–30.
66. Matt. 12:40.
67. John 2:18–19.
68. John 2:20–22.

CHAPTER EIGHT

1. Matt. 27:20–23 (NRSV).
2. Mark 15:15 (NRSV).
3. *The HarperCollins Study Bible*, op. cit., page 2049, ft. 19.1.
4. Isa. 53:5. See I Pet. 2:24.
5. Matt. 27:27–31 (NRSV).
6. Isa. 53:3.
7. I Pet. 2:21.
8. John 19:16–17 (NRSV).
9. Luke 23:26 (NRSV).
10. Luke 23:33–34 (NRSV).
11. Luke 23:35–38 (NRSV).
12. Luke 23:39–43 (NRSV).
13. John 19:25–27 (NRSV).
14. Mark 15:33–34 (NRSV).
15. See John 20:24–28 where Jesus showed his nail-scarred hands to
    Thomas.
16. John 19:28–30 (NRSV).
17. Luke 23:46 (NRSV).
18. Mark 15:39 (NRSV).
19. John 19:31–34 (NRSV).
20. *The HarperCollins Study Bible*, op. cit., page 2051, ft. 19.31–33.
21. Mark 15:43–46 (NRSV).
22. Matt. 27:62–66 (NRSV).
23. John 12:27. (NRSV)
24. John 18:11.
25. Luke 22:42. See also Mark 14:36 and Matt. 26:39, 42.
26. Matt. 17:22–23 (NASB). See also Matt. 16:21; Mark 8:31 and Luke
    9:22.
27. Mark 9:30–31 (NASB).
28. Matt. 12:38–40.

29. John 2:18–22.
30. Mark 14:50 (NASB). See also Matt. 26:56.
31. Mark 16:1–3 (NASB).
32. Matt. 28:2–8 (NASB).
33. John 20:14–18.
34. John 20:3–7 (NASB).
35. John 20:8–9 (NASB).
36. John 19:33; Mark 15:42–45.
37. Matt. 27:62–66.
38. Acts 10:39–41.
39. II Pet. 1:16–18; I John 1:1–3.
40. William Alva Gifford, *The Story of the Faith*, (NY: The Macmillan Company, 1946), pp. 118–119.
41. Tacitus, *Annals IV*, xxxiii–xliv, as quoted in Gifford, ibid., p. 118.
42. Mireille Hadas–Level, *Flavius Josephus, Eyewitness to Rome's First-Century Conquest of Judea*, Translation by Richard Miller (NY: Macmillan Publishing Company, 1993).
43. Ibid., p. 229.
44. Flavius Josephus, *Antiquities of the Jews*, Book XVIII, Chapter III, paragraph 3, Translation by William Whiston (Grand Rapids, MI: Kregel Publications, 1981), p. 379.
45. Chadwick, op. cit., page 235.
46. Cruden, op. cit., page 290.
47. Rom. 10:9–10 (NAB), emphasis added. See also Acts 8:37.
48. John Cardinal O'Connor, Archbishop of NY, quoted in "Who Was Jesus?" *Life Magazine*, December, 1994, p. 71.
49. Parts of the foregoing are taken from the author's *The Choices Are Yours*, (Highland City, FL: Rainbow Books, 1998), pages 99–102.
50. Gen. 22:8.
51. Gen. 22:13.
52. John 1:29.
53. John 1:36.
54. See Leviticus Chapters 4–5; and Leviticus 6:1–7.
55. Lev. 17:11.
56. Matt. 20:28; Mark 10:45.
57. Rom. 3:23–24.
58. I Pet. 2:24 (NASB).
59. I Pet. 1:18–19 (NASB).

CHAPTER NINE

1. Mark 1:14–15 (NASB). See also Matt. 4:17.
2. Luke 4:43 (NASB). emphasis added.
3. Luke 8:1 (NASB).
4. Luke 9:1–2 (NASB).
5. Luke 10:1, 9 (NASB).
6. Isa. 9:7. Cf. Matt. 22:42 and Luke 1:32–33.
7. Isa. 11:4–5.
8. Isa. 9:7.
9. Isa. 9:7; 11:6–9.
10. Isa. 11:2.
11. Ps. 145:13.
12. Dan. 2:44. Parenthetical explanation added.
13. Dan. 7:13–14.
14. Dan. 7:18.
15. Dan. 12:2.
16. Matt. 27:37 (NASB).
17. Acts 1:6.
18. Matt. 8:11. Parenthetical explanation added. Cf. Luke 13:28–29; Matt. 21:33–45.
19. John 4:24 (NASB).
20. John 18:36.
21. Luke 17:20–21 (NASB).
22. Mark 4:30 (NASB). And see Luke 13:18, 20.
23. Mark 4:10–12 (NASB). And see Luke 8:10.
24. Matt. 13:16–17 (NASB). See likewise Luke 10:23–24.
25. Luke 10:21.
26. Ps. 89:14 (NASB).
27. Matt. 6:25–33 (NASB). See also Luke 12:31.
28. Matt. 13:44–46 (NASB).
29. Luke 10:17, 20.
30. Matt. 13:24–30 (NASB).
31. Matt. 13:36–43 (NASB).
32. Matt. 13:47–50 (NASB).
33. Matt. 25:31–46 (NASB).
34. Ibid., v. 34.
35. Ibid., v. 46.
36. Matt. 5:20.
37. Matt. 23:1–33.

38. Matt. 8:12. See where John the Baptist said they must "bring forth fruits meet for repentance" because their reliance on Abraham was not enough. Matt. 3:7–10. See also Luke 13:23–30.
39. Matt. 21:23–32. See also the parable of the lord of the vineyard which followed in Matt. 21:33–45.
40. Luke 9:59–62.
41. Matt. 18:3.
42. Matt. 25:31–46.
43. Matt. 6:14–15; Matt. 18:21–35; Mark 11:25–26.
44. I Cor. 6:9–10 (NASB). Paul lists fornicators, idolaters, adulterers, effeminate, homosexuals, thieves, the covetous, drunkards, revilers, and swindlers.
45. John 3:3, 5; I Cor. 15:50.
46. Matt. 19:23–24; Luke 18:24–25.
47. Mark 10:24–25.
48. Matt. 6:19–21 (NASB).
49. See I Tim. 6:10 (NASB) where Paul writes ". . . the love of money is a root of all sorts of evil, . . .".
50. Luke 12:35–48.
51. Luke 12:19–20.
52. Matt. 25:1–13.

CHAPTER TEN

1. John 3:3.
2. John 2:23.
3. John 3:2–7 (NASB).
4. John 3:12 (NASB).
5. En route to Canaan from Egypt the people were bitten by serpents, and many died. At God's direction, Moses made a bronze serpent and set it on a pole. Then any who were bitten looked up to the bronze serpent, and lived. See Num. 21:4–9. And see John 12:32–33, where Jesus refers to his being "lifted up" as meaning his crucifixion.
6. John 3:14–18 (NASB).
7. Mark 10:14–15. And see Luke 18:16–17.
8. John 3:5–6 (NASB).
9. C. S. Lewis, *Surprised by Joy*, (NY: Harcourt Brace & Company, a Harvest Book, 1955), page 218.
10. Ibid., page 220.
11. Mark 1:14–15.
12. Ibid., and see Mark 16:15–16.

13. *The American Heritage Dictionary*, op. cit., page 568.
14. *Oxford Companion to the Bible*, op. cit., page 258.
15. Robert Young, *Analytical Concordance to the Bible*, 22nd American Ed., Revised by William B. Stevenson, (NY: Funk & Wagnalls Co.), page 430.
16. Cruden, op. cit., p. 265.
17. I Pet. 4:17; Rom. 1:1; 15:16; I Thes. 2:2, 8, 9.
18. Rom. 1:16; I Cor. 9:12, 18; II Cor. 2:12.
19. Rom. 10:15; Eph. 6:15.
20. Mark 1:14. But see the NASB translation where it is called simply "the gospel of God".
21. Matt. 24:14.
22. John 14:1. Cf. John 6:29; 11:25–26.
23. John 1:11–13. (Parenthetical explanation added.)
24. John 6:24, 26, 32 (NASB).
25. John 6:35 (NASB).
26. John 6:40 (NASB).
27. John 7:37–39 (NASB).
28. John 14:11.
29. Acts 8:37–38.
30. Acts 10:43.
31. Acts 16:31.
32. John 7:16–17 (NASB).
33. Mark 1:14–15.
34. Luke 9:23–24. And see Matt. 16:24–25; Mark 8:34–35.
35. Matt. 10:38–39.
36. Rom. 10:8–10 (NASB).
37. See John 12:42–43 where he writes of those who were afraid of being "put out of the synagogue". And Jesus warned us: "whosoever therefore shall be ashamed of me and of my words in this adulterous and sinful generation; of him also shall the Son of man be ashamed, when he cometh in the glory of his Father with the holy angels." Mark 8:38. And see Luke 9:26.
38. Matt. 5:11–12 (NASB). And see Luke 6:22–23.
39. Matt. 18:4.
40. Luke 6:44–45 (NASB). To the same effect, see Matt. 7:18–19.
41. John 15:1–2, 4–6, 8 (NASB).
42. Matt. 13:23 (NASB). See also Mark 4:3–20; Luke 8:15.
43. Matt. 5:27–28.
44. Luke 12:15.
45. Matt. 5:21–22.

46. Matt. 25:31–46.
47. Luke 14:12–14.
48. Rom. 13:8–10 (NASB).
49. Gal. 5:22–23 (NASB).
50. Eph. 5:9.
51. Matt. 6:1–6, 16–18.
52. Luke 14:7–11.
53. Luke 22:24–27.
54. Matt. 20:20–28; Mark 10:35–45.
55. John 3:16–21.
56. Luke 15:11–32.
57. Luke 15:4–10.

CHAPTER ELEVEN

1. See Acts 15:1–6; Rom. 2:25–29; 4:7–13; Col. 3:9–11.
2. Gal. 2:11–14.
3. Acts 11:1–18
4. Justo L. Gonzalez, *The Story of Christianity*, (NY: HarperCollins Publishers, 1984), Vol. 1, pages 53–56.
5. Gifford, op. cit., pages 155–159.
6. Ibid., page 172.
7. Hugh Thomas, *World History, Revised Edition*, (NY: HarperCollins, 1996), page 161. Submitted excerpt from *World History* by Hugh Thomas Copyright © 1996 by Hugh Thomas. Reprinted by permission of HarperCollins Publishers, Inc.
8. Daniel B. Clendenin, *Eastern Orthodox Christianity*, (Grand Rapids, MI: Baker Books, 1994), pages 40–41.
9. Mary Jo Weaver, *Introduction to Christianity*, (Belmont, CA: Wadsworth Publishing Company, 1984), page 64.
10. Justo L. Gonzalez, *The Story of Christianity*, (NY: HarperCollins Publishers, 1985), Vol. 2, page 15.
11. *Catechism*, op. cit., § 1129, page 319, citing Council of Trent (1547).
12. *Catechism*, op. cit., §§ 979–987, pages 277–279. This is still Roman Catholic doctrine.
13. Thomas, op. cit., page 233.
14. Ibid.
15. Ibid., page 468.
16. Charles Van Doren, *A History of Knowledge*, (NY: Ballantine Books, 1991), page 167.

17. Gifford, op. cit., page 344.
18. Richard Marius, *Martin Luther: The Christian Between God and Death*, (Cambridge, Mass: The Belknap Press of Harvard University Press, 1999), page 387.
19. *Catechism*, op. cit., §§ 81–82, page 31.
20. Ibid., § 85, page 32.
21. Frank S. Mead, *Handbook of Denominations in the United States*, 10th Ed., Rev. by Samuel S. Hill, (Nashville: Abingdon Press, 1995), page 174.
22. Ibid.
23. Ibid, emphasis added.
24. Gifford, op. cit., page 360–361.
25. Ibid., page 362.
26. Ibid., page 366.
27. Mead, op. cit., page 261. See also Lefferts A. Loetscher, *A Brief History of the Presbyterians*, 4th Ed. (Philadelphia: The Westminster Press, 1983), pages 23–28.
28. Gonzalez, op. cit., Vol. 2, page 72.
29. *The Papal Encyclicals in Their Historical Context*, Ann Fremantle, Editor (NY: A Mentor Book, The New American Library of World Literature, Inc., 1956), page 83.
30. Ibid., page 82.
31. *The Confession of Faith*, (Richmond, VA: The Presbyterian Church in the United States, 1965), pages 8–9.
32. Mark A Noll, *A History of Christianity in the United States and Canada*, (Grand Rapids, MI: William B. Eerdmans Publishing Co., 1992), pages 32–33; Weaver, op cit., pages 97–98, 107.
33. See "The Origin and Formation of the Westminster Confession of Faith" in *The Confession of Faith of the Presbyterian Church in the United States*, (Richmond, VA: The Board of Christian Education, 1965), page 13.
34. F. E. Halliday, *England, a Concise History*, (London: Thames and Hudson, Ltd., 1989), page 115. He was speaking of William Laud, who became Archbishop of Canterbury.
35. Loetscher, op. cit., pages 49–51.
36. William H. Brackney, *The Baptists*, (Westport, Conn: Praeger Publishers, 1994), page ix.
37. Ibid., page 5.
38. See Fremantle, op cit., pages 77–80, and Noll, op. cit., page 13.
39. Barry A. Kosmin and Seymour P. Lachman, *One Nation Under God*, (NY: Harmony Books, 1993), page 19. See also Justo L. Gonzalez

in *World Religions in America*, Jacob Neusner, Ed., (Louisville, KY: Westminster/John Knox Press, 1994), pages 111–112.

40. Mead., op. cit., page 270; U.S. Bureau of the Census, *Statistical Abstract of the United States 1997*, Table 2, page 8, compared with Table 85, page 69.

41. From Jefferson's autobiography in Maureen Harrison & Steve Gilbert Editors, *Thomas Jefferson In His Own Words*, (NY: Barnes & Noble Books, 1996), page 191.

42. Winthrop S. Hudson and John Corrigan, *Religion in America*, 5th Ed., (NY: Macmillan Publishing Co., 1992), page 32.

43. Paul Johnson, *A History of the American People*, (NY: HarperCollins Publishers, 1997), page 53.

44. Allan Nevins and Henry Steele Commager, *A Short History of the United States*, (NY: Random House, 1956), page 24.

45. Ola Elizabeth Winslow, *Samuel Sewall of Boston*, (NY: The Macmillan Co. 1964), page 90.

46. Ibid., page 92. See also Hudson and Corrigan, op. cit., page 33.

47. Mead, op. cit., pages 285, 291.

48. Loetscher, op. cit., page 59.

49. Hudson and Corrigan, op. cit., pages 44–45.

50. Bryan F. LeBeau, *Jonathan Dickinson and the Formative Years of American Presbyterianism*, (Lexington, KY: The University Press of Kentucky, 1997), page 65.

51. Ibid., pages 27 et seq.

52. Ibid., pages 37–38.

53. J. M. Carroll, *The Trail of Blood*, (Lexington, KY: Ashland Avenue Baptist Church, 1931).

54. Mead, op. cit., pages 49–55; Weaver, op. cit., pages 98, 107.

55. Brackney, op. cit., pages 10–11. See also Winthrop S. Hudson, *Religion in America*, 3rd Ed., (NY: Charles Scribner's Sons, 1981), page 44.

56. Carroll, op. cit., page 48.

57. U.S. Bureau of the Census, op. cit., Table 85, page 69.

58. Arthur Emery Farnsley II, *Southern Baptist Politics*, (University Park, PA: The Pennsylvania State University Press, 1994), pages x–xiii.

59. Ibid., pages 85–86, 107, 120–121.

60. Percy Livingstone Parker, Editor, *The Journal of John Wesley*, (Chicago: Moody Press), pages 46–47,

61. Ibid., pages 48–51.

62. Mead, op. cit., pages 194–195. See also Weaver, op. cit., pages 102–103.

63. Gonzalez, op. cit., Vol. 2, page 214. See also *The Journal of John Wesley*, op. cit., pages 149 and 159, which tell of two experiences with mobs.
64. Hudson and Corrigan, op. cit., page 124.
65. Weaver, op. cit., page 122. For the views of the Pentecostals compared with those of the Methodists and others, see Dieter, op. cit.
66. See Vinson Synan, "William Seymour," in *Christian History*, Vol. XIX, No. 1, Feb. 2000.
67. See Paul Prather, *Modern-Day Miracles* (Kansas City: Andrews and McMeel, 1996), page 157, where Prather quotes a 1995 survey which revealed "that 11 percent of U.S. adults say they have asked God to give them the ability to speak in tongues, and 7 percent have received the gift."
68. Ibid., page 161.
69. U.S. Bureau of the Census, op. cit., Table 85, page 69.

CHAPTER TWELVE

1. U.S. Bureau of the Census, op. cit., Table No. 85, page 69.
2. Mead, op. cit., Appendix D, pages 308–316.
3. Duncan Ferguson, *Biblical Hermeneutics*, (Atlanta: John Knox Press, 1986), pages 6–7.
4. Ibid., page 18.
5. Robert M. Grant, *A Short History of the Interpretation of the Bible*, Rev. Ed., (NY: The Macmillan Company, 1963), page 84.
6. Ibid., page 129.
7. Ibid., page 177.
8. Bart D. Ehrman, *The New Testament: A Historical Introduction to the Early Christian Writings*, 2nd Ed., (NY: Oxford University Press, 2000), page 14. Parenthetical explanation added.
9. James L. Kugel, *The Bible as it Was*, (Cambridge, MA: The Belknap Press of Harvard University Press, 1997), pages 4–5.
10. Norman L. Geisler, *Christian Apologetics*, (Grand Rapids, MI: Baker Book House, 1997), page 307.
11. Hershel Shanks, Editor, *Understanding the Dead Sea Scrolls*, (NY: Random House, 1992), page xix.
12. Ibid., page 183.
13. John 7:53 through 8:11.
14. John 4:20.
15. John 4:21, 23–24 (NASB).

16. Micah 6:7–8 (NASB). Parenthetical explanatory word added.
17. Claude G. Bowers, *Jefferson and Hamilton*, (Chautauqua, NY: The Chautauqua Press, 1927), pages 103–104.
18. Fawn M. Brodie, *Thomas Jefferson, An Intimate History*, (NY: W. W. Norton & Company, 1974), page 129.
19. Ibid., page 326.
20. Max Beloff, *Thomas Jefferson and American Democracy*, (NY: Collier Books, 1962), page 71. See also Noble E. Cunningham, Jr., *In Pursuit of Reason*, Baton Rouge, LA: Louisiana State University Press, 1987), pages 55, 58.
21. Howard Elmo Short, quoted in Brochure from Old Cane Ridge Meeting-house, Bourbon County, Kentucky. For Stone's autobiography, see Hoke S Dickinson, Editor, *The Cane Ridge Reader*, (Paris, KY: Cane Ridge Preservation Project, 1972)
22. William Clayton Bower, *Central Christian Church, Lexington, Kentucky, A History*, (St. Louis: The Bethany Press, 1962), pages 23–24.
23. *The Cane Ridge Reader*, op. cit.
24. Adron Doran, *Restoring New Testament Christianity*, (Nashville: 21st Century Christian, 1997), page 66.
25. Ibid., pages 68, 110.
26. Noll, op. cit., page 151.
27. Bower, op. cit., page 25.
28. Doran, op. cit., pages 36–37.
29. Ibid., page 110.
30. Bower, op. cit., page 43; Mead, op. cit., page 98; Doran, op. cit., page 110.
31. John 17:20–23, emphasis added.
32. Emerson Colaw, *Beliefs of a United Methodist Christian*, (Nashville: Tidings, 1972), page 11.
33. Ibid., page 14.
34. Loetscher, op. cit., page 171.
35. I Cor. 14:34–35 (NASB).
36. John 14:16–17; 16:13.
37. Exod. 20:7.
38. Doran, op. cit., pages 36–37.
39. Mead, op. cit., page 211.
40. Edwin A. Sawyer, *All About the Moravians*, (Bethlehem, PA: The Moravian Church in America, 1990), page 4.
41. Mead, op. cit., page 210, and Sawyer, ibid., page 74.

CHAPTER THIRTEEN

1. William J. Gaither, Alexandria, IN (1970).
2. Dan. 7:13–14 (NASB).
3. Mark 14:61–62 (NRSV). See likewise Matt. 26:63–64 and Luke 22:67–69.
4. Matt. 26:65–68; Mark 14:63–65; Luke 22:71.
5. Matt. 24:29–31 (NRSV). See also Mark 13:24–27 and Luke 21:25–27.
6. John 14:1–3 (NASB).
7. Matt. 6:9–13.
8. Acts 1:9–11 (NRSV).
9. I Thes. 4:16–17 (NASB).
10. J. R. Dummelow, Editor, *A Commentary on the Holy Bible*, (NY: The Macmillan Company, 1955), page 1066.
11. Rev. 20:4–6 (NRSV).
12. Rev. 20:7–10 (NRSV).
13. Rev. 20:11–15 (NRSV).
14. Rev. 21:1–4 (NRSV), emphasis added.
15. Jer. 31:31–34, emphasis added.
16. Ezek. 36:25–28, emphasis added.
17. Ezek. 37:26.
18. Matt. 26:28. And see Mark 14:24; Luke 22:20; I Cor. 11:25.
19. Eph. 2:13–18 (NASB).
20. I Cor. 2:11–14 (NASB).
21. John 1:12–13 (NASB).
22. I Cor. 12:1–31.
23. Gal. 5:16–26.
24. Eph. 6:10–17.
25. Luke 17:21 (NASB). The King James Version translates this as "the kingdom of God is within you", and the New Revised Standard Version as "the kingdom of God is among you". All are in the present tense.
26. *Catechism*, op. cit., § 541, pages 152–153.
27. Ibid., § 680, page 195.
28. Ibid., § 816, page 234.
29. Encyclical issued August 10, 1863, by Pope Pius IX, quoted by Anne Fremantle in *The Papal Encyclicals in Their Historical Context*, op. cit., page 132.
30. *Catechism*, op. cit., § 818, page 235.
31. Doran, op. cit., page 17.

32. Eph. 1:22–23; Col. 1:24; I Cor. 12:27.
33. Matt. 13:23 (NASB).
34. Matt. 13:33 (NASB).
35. Matt. 13:19.
36. Matt. 13:23.
37. Herschel H. Hobbs, *What Baptists Believe*, (Nashville: Broadman Press, 1964), page 117.
38. Henry, *Fundamentals of the Faith*, op. cit., page 259.

CHAPTER FOURTEEN

1. Mead, op. cit., page 34.
2. Ibid., page 37.
3. Keith J. Hardman, *Issues in American Christianity*, (Grand Rapids, MI: Baker Books, 1993), page 151.
4. Hal Lindsey, *Planet Earth 2000 A.D.*, (Palos Verdes, CA: Western Front, Ltd., 1996), unnumbered third page of Introduction.
5. Ibid., pages 173–174.
6. Ibid., page 309.
7. Ibid., page 310.
8. Ibid., page 311.
9. Ibid., page 312.
10. Ray W. Yerbury, *Vital Signs of Christ's Return*, (Green Forest, AR: New Leaf Press, Inc., 1995).
11. Ibid., pages 45–46.
12. Ibid., page 46.
13. Ibid., page 149.
14. Ibid., page 150.
15. Ed Dobson, *The End: Why Jesus Could Return by A.D. 2000*, (Grand Rapids, MI: Zondervan Publishing House, 1997).
16. Ibid., page 37. See Yerbury, op. cit., page 32.
17. Ibid., page 167.
18. Ibid., page 167.
19. Ibid., page 167.
20. Ibid., pages 151–163.
21. Thomas Robbins and Susan J. Palmer, Editors, *Millennium, Messiahs, and Mayhem: Contemporary Apocalyptic Movements*, (NY: Routledge, 1997), page 4.
22. Ibid., pages 22–23.

23. Laurie Goodstein, "Novel on Rapture utilizes God's word, Clancy's style", *Lexington Herald-Leader*, October 4, 1998, page A2, and continued on page A12.

24. Ibid.

25. Ibid.

26. Margaret Nutting Ralph, *The Bible and the End of the World: Should We Be Afraid?*, (Mahwah, NJ: Paulist Press, 1997), page 163.

27. Ibid., pages 14–15.

28. Ibid., page 133.

29. Ibid., page 163.

30. Clark Morphew, "If the end is coming, I'd better plan now", *Lexington Herald-Leader*, November 21, 1998, page C–10, and continued on page C–8.

31. Ibid., page C–8.

32. Matt. 24:34–36 (NASB). Compare Mark 13:30–32; Luke 21:32. The marginal notes in the NASB offer "race" as an alternative to the word translated "generation" in the text.

33. Matt. 16:28 (NASB).

34. Matt. 24:14 (NASB).

35. *Master Study Bible, (NASB)*, (Nashville: Holman Bible Publishers, 1981), marginal notes to Matt. 24:34, Mark 13:30 and Luke 21:32.

36. *The New American Bible*, (Grand Rapids, MI: World Publishing, 1991) See marginal note to Matt. 24:34 which says: "The difficulty raised by this verse cannot be satisfactorily removed by the supposition that *this generation* means the Jewish people throughout the course of their history, much less the entire human race. Perhaps for Matthew it means the *generation* to which he and his community belonged."

37. C. S. Lewis, *The World's Last Night*, (San Diego: Harcourt Brace & Company, A Harvest Book: 1987), pages 98–99.

38. II Thes. 2:1–5.

39. II Thes. 2:3–10.

40. Matt. 24:36–39 (NAB). See also Mark 13:32.

41. Mark 13:33–37 (NAB).

42. Ezek. 3:17–19; see likewise Ezek. 33:7–9.

43. II Pet. 3:3–9 (NASB), emphasis added.

44. II Pet. 3:13 (NASB).

45. James 5:7–8 (NASB).

46. John Naisbitt and Patricia Aburdene, *Megatrends 2000*, (NY: William Morrow and Company, Inc., 1990), page 270.

47. Ibid., page 297.

CHAPTER FIFTEEN

1. Matt. 7:21–27 (NASB).
2. James 2:14–18 (NASB).
3. Eph. 2:8–9 (NASB).
4. Matt. 21:28–32 (RSV) Parenthetical reference added.
5. Matt. 13:31–32 (NASB).
6. John 14:15–17.
7. John 14:26.
8. John 15:26–27.
9. John 16:13.
10. Heb. 8:8–12; 10:16–17.
11. Matt. 5:17–19.
12. Rom. 2:13–16 (NAB).
13. Rom. 3:20. See also Rom. 7:7.
14. II Cor. 3:6 (NASB).
15. Mark 3:4. See also Luke 6:6–10.
16. See Luke 13:11–17; 14:1–6; John 5:1–18; 7:23; 9:13–16.
17. Mark 2:27–28. See also Luke 6:1–5.
18. Luke 11:42 (NASB).
19. Luke 11:46 (NASB).
20. Luke 12:1 (NASB).
21. Matt. 12:35; Luke 6:45.
22. Cruden, op. cit., p. 290.
23. Rom:13:8.
24. The talent was a unit of money, the value of which was relatively high but depended on whether it was gold, silver, or some baser metal. See ft. to Matt. 18:24 in the New American Bible.
25. Matt. 25:24–30 (NAB). See also a similar parable in Luke 19:11–27.
26. Matt. 25:31–46.
27. John 15:1–2, 4–5, 8 (NASB), emphasis added.
28. Gal. 5:22–23.
29. Eph. 5:9.
30. Matt. 13:33 (NASB).
31. Matt. 5:13.
32. Matt. 5:14; John 8:12.
33. John 4:14.
34. Matt. 5:13; Luke 14:34; Mark 9:50.
35. Matt. 5:15–16; Mark 4:21; Luke 8:16; 11:33.

36. Luke 17:1–2 (NRSV). See also Matt. 18:6–7 where the example we set for children is emphasized.
37. John 4:35–38 (NASB).
38. Luke 10:2 (NASB).
39. Mark 1:17.
40. Mark 16:15–16.
41. Rom. 10:13–15.
42. Mark 4:26–29.
43. See above comments concerning John 4:35–38.
44. See John 6:44 where Jesus said, "No man can come to me, except the Father which hath sent me draw him . . ."
45. Luke 13:6–9 (NASB).
46. Matt. 25:21.

CONCLUSIONS

1. Rev. 22:17. (NAB)
2. I Cor. 13:9–10, 12. (NASB)
3. I Cor. 2:14.
4. McGrath, op. cit., page 24.
5. John Shelby Spong, *Born of a Woman*, (San Francisco: Harper San Francisco, 1992), page 5.
6. Ibid., page 9.
7. Ibid., page xvi.
8. They point to Mark 16:18 and Acts 28:3–6.
9. But see I Cor. 14:1–40.
10. Mark 13:7; Matt. 24:6.
11. Mark 13:8; Matt. 24:7.
12. See, for example, the blessings of Paul. Rom. 15:33 and Heb. 13:20–21.
13. Rom. 10:8–10.
14. Matt. 28:19–20.
15. Heb. 13:20–21.

To order additional copies of

THE

BRIDGE

OF

FAITH

have your credit card ready and call

(877) 421-READ (7323)

or send $15.95 each + $4.95* S&H to

**WinePress Publishing
PO Box 428
Enumclaw, WA 98022**

www.winepresspub.com

*add $2.00 S&H for each additional book ordered